T0328552

DIALECTIC OF ENLIGHTENMENT
AS SPORT

DIALECTIC OF ENLIGHTENMENT AS SPORT

The Barbaric Urge
within
Sports, Religion, and Capitalism

TOM DONOVAN

Algora Publishing
New York

Library of Congress Cataloging-in-Publication Data —

Donovan, Tom, 1967–
    Dialectic of enlightenment as sport: The barbaric urge within sports, religion, and
Capitalism / Tom Donovan.
        pages cm
    Includes bibliographical references and index.
    ISBN 978-1-62894-162-3 (soft cover: alk. paper) — ISBN 978-1-62894-163-0 (hard
cover: alk. paper) ISBN 978-1-62894-164-7 (eBook) 1. Horkheimer, Max, 1895–1973.
Philosophische Fragmente. 2. Adorno, Theodor W., 1903–1969. 3. Philosophy. 4. Sports—
Philosophy. I. Title.
    B3279.H8473P534 2015
    193—dc23
                        2015026714

Cover illustration by Wendy Walczak.

Printed in the United States

For Christine and Thomas

SPORT:

Physical activity engaged in for pleasure
To amuse oneself
To stray from style
To satirize

Table of Contents

TEBOW TIME

It was hard not to believe that God was rooting for Tim Tebow on that glorious January day in 2012 when the Denver Broncos defeated the Pittsburgh Steelers.[1] Denver had suffered humiliating losses in their previous three football games and limped into the playoffs. Tebow himself seemed off his game as he struggled to complete even the simplest quarterback duties. Then, suddenly, in the quickest overtime in NFL history, Tebow threw a beautiful pass to a cutting Demaryius Thomas, who raced 80 yards to the end zone. With the touchdown Denver won their first playoff game in years. The "Mile High Messiah," as some called Tebow, ran towards the goal post, dropped into a genuflection, his signature pose, did a fist pound, and jumped around with ecstasy throughout his victory lap. Tebow had no doubt that God had helped with this one. He thanked the Lord as soon as he saw Thomas cross the goal line and then "got on a knee and thanked the Lord again."[2]

Apparently, more Americans than not believe that God helps Tebow win football games.[3] The game itself has a Wikipedia page where it is known as the "3:16 game."[4] John 3:16 is Tebow's favorite bible verse and his epic playoff win has an eerie number of numerical associations to it. The total yards Tebow passed the football that day, the average yards per reception, the game's television ratings, the Steelers' time of possession, all contain 3:16 in some form.[5] In response to all this,

---

1 The Denver Broncos beat the Pittsburgh Steelers on January 8th 2012. Tebow threw the winning pass in overtime.
2 http://scores.espn.go.com/nfl/recap?gameId=320108007
3 http://www.csmonitor.com/USA/Sports/2012/0112/Poll-God-helps-Tim-Tebow-win-football-games.-Does-Tim-Tebow-agree
4 http://en.wikipedia.org/wiki/3:16_Game
5 Ibid.

Twitter broke twitting records and Google searches of this New Testament verse hit an all-time high. The urge to find metaphysical significance seems to extend from the local church to the sports field and even into the cyber world.

Still, Tebow himself doesn't seem to want or expect God to help him win. Rather he appears to be motivated by intrinsic values, and his focus seems to be on keeping his character and soul pure. Even when the game is on the line he has been heard saying: "Dear Jesus, I need you. Please come through for me. No matter what happens, win or lose, give me the strength to honor you,"[1] and, "Lord put a wall of protection around me and my teammates today, and we go out there and we can honor you with everything we do and say. I love you in Jesus' name."[2] And despite losing the next playoff game, and eventually losing his NFL job, Tebow has remained positive and grounded, and his popularity has not dissipated. For we live in the Age of Tebowing.

1 http://www.csmonitor.com/USA/Sports/2012/0112/Poll-God-helps-Tim-Tebow-win-football-games.-Does-Tim-Tebow-agree
2 Ibid.

INTRODUCTION. SCHIZOPHRENIC MODERNITY

One could half-seriously ask if Max Horkheimer and Theodor Adorno might find themselves rooting for Tim Tebow. Although, from all indications, these German philosophers were not fans of American football, today they might find themselves rooting for someone or something pushing back against actual existing modernity. In a world that has become increasingly cynical and economically calculating, two guys, who more than half a century ago already thought instrumental reason had become totalitarian, might have to get behind someone who seems to be guided by an intrinsic and metaphysical impulse.

Does Tim Tebow represent a challenge to the period called Modernity? Where else could one find such a competitive other of reason, such a force of nature? How dare coaches and football experts *a priori* determine what it means to be a quarterback when God is on Tebow's team? Tebow's popularity, success, and faith seem to offer a counterexample to the idea that in modernity victory, progress, success, and happiness require strategic conniving, scientific and technological advantage, progressive ideas, and the privatization of religion. For whether we are talking about Kant's injunction that enlightenment means: "*Sapere aude!* Have the courage to use your own reason,"[1] or the *Communist Manifesto*'s confidence that "man is at last compelled to face with sober senses, his real conditions of life,"[2] modernity, with its iron clad, self-reflective rationality, relentlessly conceived of itself as beyond and superior to tradition, faith, and external authority. Even Habermas declared that: "Modernity can and will no

---

1 Kant, "What is Enlightenment" in *Foundations of the Metaphysics of Morals*, Lewis White Beck tr. (New Jersey: Prentice-Hall, 1997) 83.
2 Marx, "The Communist Manifesto" in *The Marx-Engels Reader*, Robert C. Tucker ed. (New York: Norton, 1978.) 476.

longer borrow the criteria by which it takes its orientation from the models supplied by another epoch; *it has to create its normativity out of itself.*"[1] Yet steel could not defeat prayer. The only ones compelled to face reality with sober senses turned out to be the Pittsburgh Steelers, and they also were full of tears and lacking in orientation, victory, success, progress, and happiness when Tebow finished with them. How strange are the times we live in if Tebow's success and popularity seem to validate Horkheimer and Adorno's warning of the return and revenge of the Other of enlightenment reason, as well as their skepticism towards the modern project in general?

As the Tebow phenomenon shows, the world that the Enlightenment was supposed to usher in turns out not to be sufficient for winning football games, grounding normativity, or giving humans something meaningful to believe in. And as we clearly know now, but perhaps don't like to admit, the Scientific Revolution and the Enlightenment themselves were deeply intertwined with superstition and faith, and these sacred impulses still have not melted into air. Metaphysical urges are hard to shake. In the world we live in today it is more than common to link one's idea of individual progress or social hope with some sort of non-human inspiration. It's difficult to rely solely on self-reflective reason or the merely human. It's unclear whether modernity can ever shake the pull of the transcendent, but that is not to say that people today completely trust their faith and pre-modern ideologies either. As the joke the Aunt tells in Woody Allen's *Crimes and Misdemeanors* captures: a boxer's corner asks a Priest to pray for their fighter and the Priest says he will, but continues with "it will help if he can punch!" In our world, many may still pray, but they also learn how to punch. Science and reason have not destroyed superstition and faith, and those who adhere to ancient myths don't typically reject all of modernity.

In the case of Tebow, his magical year did not lead to a second coming.[2] God has not unambiguously blessed him. Tebow is once again under the sway of material and market forces. And Tebow is not just counting on faith to get through it. Rather the Tebow way of being does not completely reject the progress modernity has afforded us. Tebow uses the latest technology, equipment, trainers, coaches, and cutting edge training methods to hone his craft, and in his mind, not at the expense of his religious and metaphysical beliefs. He's joined forces with a prominent agent[3] to extend his brand beyond playing football. In fact Tebow exemplifies a new brand of Christian warrior walking the streets of America today. This species does not shun

---

1 Jürgen Habermas, *The Philosophical Discourse* of *Modernity*, Frederick Lawrence, tr. (The MIT Press Cambridge, Massachusetts 1992) 7.
2 Although thanks to Tebow's relentless hard work and dedication, and Chip Kelly's ego, Tebow has a legitimate shot at making the Philadelphia Eagles.
3 Nick Khan

the perks and gadgets of the profane modern world. One does not have to market himself as a naturalist Rocky training in nature's pure white snow[1] while an artificial, steroid shooting, cyborg-like man from Russia uses ultra-modern training tools and propaganda to try to beat you into submission. Rather, today's Christian is a teched-out warrior on twitter. Go into any megachurch today and you will find God's people logging into Facebook, see the congregation's youth downloading Christian rock or rap, and watch the bible club exchanging tweets proving God's existence—or even meeting to practice MMA submission techniques. Likewise, with Tebow, we saw a modern, rational, and calculating football player fused with ancient, faith-based beliefs and actions: wild animal aggression in Nike cleats running to the goal line transformed into a gentle pious Tebowing in the end zone, a chiseled Wolverine body with bible verses extolling love under the eyes, a self-proclaimed virgin who hangs with and dates celebrities. And if and when the football is over it won't halt the Tebow crusade. Religion can be found in all corners of our modern, capitalist culture so there will always be a place in modernity for Tebow's ilk. And if the college football announcing doesn't work out one could imagine Tebow getting an online offer to sell his virginity to the highest bidder with the proceeds going to build a church in some depraved part of the world. But for now, Tebow and T-Mobile have teamed up, and the sacred and the profane have never been more intimate.

Tebow's success and struggles makes it clear that the modern world is an ambiguous world in which it is hard to even adequately grasp, conceptualize, define, or understand. The world is becoming more and more profane, secular, and strategic, and at the same time, religion has come back like a force of nature. It is a world that embraces both "The Wolf of Wall Street" and the "Jesus Freak."[2] It is a world that seems to have paradoxically given us progress and decline at the same time, and from both ends of the spectrum.

On the one hand, we are the recipients of vast advances in health, longevity, modern comforts, scientific progress, and the like. Religion has been de-centered and made more tolerant as critical thinking and rival worldviews enter the lifeworld. On the other hand though, while many of our technological advances and modern comforts serve human needs, just as many seem to distract and alienate us. And de-centered religion, while making many more tolerant, has also brought out a more irrational, frenzied, and dogmatic faith in some and a complete disenchantment with religion in others. Tolerance, moderation, and modern subjectivity are getting squeezed between a reinvigorated medieval religious conviction and a hedonistic post-

---

1 Of course, knowing what we do now about Stallone's PED use makes this especially comical.
2 This term is a badge of honor for many Christians as its prevalence on automobiles attests.

modern and pessimistic meaninglessness. Modernity seems trapped within a binary of stupid faith and senseless nihilism.

Given the salient alternatives, it is not surprising and actually almost cliché now when we see that many in the contemporary world jump with joy when a Jeremy Lin or a Tim Tebow unashamedly proclaim their faith and belief in something higher than the fad of the day, (even though they themselves are fads) and credit their success to it. It is also not surprising that it rubs a lot of people the wrong way since any metaphysical assertions seem arbitrary, deluded, or arrogant to those outside that faith. Still, it's not just the unreflective true believers who get caught up into wondering if God is actively intervening in our world (and in a football game). It's also the more skeptical and reflective folks, who in their calmer and clearer moments, may wonder and even suspect that they are clinging to an outdated and dubious metaphysics (or at least doubt that God is rooting for their favorite team) and yet in moments of stress, passion, and existential angst, suspend or compartmentalize those doubts and cheer when someone pious gets ahead in life. It seems that even, and perhaps especially, in the most modern of situations, people are looking and longing for a sign that it's a metaphysical worldview that accounts for their heroes' success and happiness. And who can blame them? Really what is the alternative? Believe in nothing, or turn rooting for the local sports team into a metaphysical event?

Horkheimer and Adorno saw this coming: "That the hygienic factory and everything pertaining to it, Volkswagen and the sports palace are... themselves becoming metaphysics...does matter." (xviii)[1] Rather than accepting a completely rationalized and demystified world people elevate sports to metaphysical status or combine them with their religion[2] to find meaning and make sense of their lives. God is not dead, not even for many philosophers. Horkheimer himself later succumbed to the sirens song of religion. Horkheimer and Adorno's *Dialectic of Enlightenment*, although firmly in the enlightenment camp, refuses to directly reject the metaphysical urge, and defends it to the extent that it may offer an intrinsic perspective and utopian promise against an increasingly instrumental and pessimistic modernity.

Non-football fans started to watch Tebow play with the hope that he could lead them to the Promised Land (or at least the Super bowl). Given how badly Tebow throws a football that would be the metaphysical sign

---

1 All page numbers in the text are from *Dialectic of Enlightenment* 2002.
2 There's even a new Christian Church called "Fight Church" where members combine worship with mixed martial arts. To quote one member: "The greatest examples in scripture of Jesus is as a fighter, that is the kind of Jesus that I would want to serve." http://www.huffingtonpost.com/2012/06/18/fight-church-documentary-_n_1605983.html. Equivocation aside, it would be delightful to see Jesus in the cage.

no one could ignore. But even if Tebow never plays another down, we can still use him as inspiration to catch that "message in a bottle" called *Dialectic of Enlightenment* (*DE* hereafter) that Horkheimer and Adorno tossed into the ocean of modernity so many years ago. *DE* was "intended to prepare a positive concept of enlightenment" (xviii) through an appeal to a negative articulation of transcendence, and we will travel into the dialectic and through the stages of Horkheimer and Adorno's text to ask if we really are, so to speak, condemned to root for Tebow.

Chapter 1. Sacrificing For The Unholy Team

Before Tebow, there was Odysseus. Before God, there were gods. In the first excursus, *DE* freely interprets Homer's *Odyssey* to continue the analysis of the intertwinement of myth and enlightenment, but now through the concepts of sacrifice and renunciation. While it is traditional to think of prayer and sacrifice as holy and intrinsic means of expression and communication, *DE* sees the notion of sacrifice as a "human contrivance intended to control the gods, who are overthrown precisely by the system created to honor them."(40) The mythic use of sacrifice that the *Odyssey* chronicles outlines a pattern and structure in which "Odysseus outwits the natural deities as the civilized traveler was later to swindle savages, offering them colored beads for ivory." (39) The moment of fraud in prayer and sacrifice is the model for cunning that develops throughout civilization. "All sacrificial acts, deliberately planned by humans, deceive the god for whom they are performed: by imposing on him the primacy of human purposes they dissolve away his power, and the fraud against him passes over seamlessly into that perpetrated by unbelieving priests against believing congregations." (40) Cunning, in those who do it well, requires a certain level of consciousness and self-consciousness: "The awareness that the symbolic communication with the deity through sacrifice was not real must have been age-old." (40) We see here that myth is already enlightenment, at least for some.

The moment of fraud is raised to self-consciousness through Odysseus, and he uses it to develop and harden himself into what Horkheimer and Adorno label a prototypical bourgeoisie. Like a good businessman whom the priest pats on the back on Sundays and thanks for his large donation, Odysseus is revered by man and god alike. Whether it is the Phaeacians, the loyal swineherd, or Penelope, everybody loves a successful guy. Athena even delights in his deception of her, and explicitly says that Odysseus's craftiness and skill in lying are why she favors him and why she is interested in protecting him.[1]

Through Odysseus we can begin to see that bourgeois exchange is just the secularization of sacrifice. But in the development of exchange, along the model of the bourgeoisie, this new self pays a price. The price is self-sacrifice in the sense that people must give up essential aspects of who they are. Just like the person whom the primitive community decides will be their sacrificial victim, the so-called enlightened self decides to sacrifice part of its being as the price to maintain its existence. The structure of fraud "which elevates the perishable person as bearer of the divine substance, has always been detectable in the ego, which owes its existence to the sacrifice of the present moment to the future." (40) Not only does the ego give something up, but this something given up is an innocent, higher, present-centered, or intrinsically good part of the self; it is the living entity. Since *DE* is an anti-theory book (it is a work of "philosophical fragments"), one simple concept will not capture the self that is lost. For the self that is sacrificed must be dialectically understood, is context dependent, and is historically and individually unique. Still, in outline, we can say it's the self that offers a promise of human happiness, the self that can achieve reconciliation with the world, others, and itself. It is the self not contaminated by supernatural fictions or instrumental domination. It is the self with the ability to not sacrifice for the future, unless harmony is maintained through ego differentiation; and as we will see, it is the self capable of tender love.

In a world of domination "deception is objectively implicit in it" (41) and so when innocents are sacrificed they are sometimes deified in order to hide the deception. But, of course, these innocents gain nothing from this honor. They do not become gods nor do they gain immortality. Rather they simply and tragically lose their lives. Likewise when one sacrifices their innocent self to succeed in a world of domination the self-deception is sold by telling oneself that their good self will sustain and will ultimately be greater when it reappears after the sacrifice. Of course, this is a lie. The self lost never returns, for it gets extinguished as the profane actions of the strategic self create a new self uninterested in the self sacrificed. At most, what is lost might occasionally be paid lip service to. For the sacrificed others perhaps we cover their coffins with the flag, play a bugle, or put a bumper sticker on the car. For the sacrificed self perhaps we give money to the guy ringing the bell outside Target in December, wear a ribbon, or hike and spa in Sedona AZ.

Ultimately though, the self that is willing to sacrifice the present for the future, the self willing to deceive and sacrifice the good, in the name of self-preservation, in so doing severs its own connection "with nature which

---

1 *The Odyssey* Book 13.

the sacrifice of the self is supposed to establish."(41) Sacrifice is supposed to keep us connected to nature, keep us in its good graces, and allow us to become what we are meant to become. Yet when the sacrifice is made simply in the name of self-preservation what we end up with is a living self that is corrupted and alienated. We end up doing to ourselves what was first imposed on helpless others. Innocent others were lied to and told that their sacrifices were necessary for survival, and we lie to ourselves that we must destroy good parts of ourselves to be successful, as we lie to others in bourgeois exchange. "Cunning is nothing other than the subjective continuation of the objective untruth of sacrifice, which it supersedes." (41)

Still, what is untruth may not have always been untruth. Sacrificing innocent victims exposes fraud but also uncovers deep and dark secrets of what humans may have had to do to survive. "In times of shortage something like cannibalism was necessary."(41) If this is true, then we can say that cunning takes hold at the split between the rational and irrational aspects of sacrifice. Cunning goes so far that we forget our embeddedness in nature, but this is partly due to nature not completely embedding us. Nature is not always kind. It does not consider our interests or needs. We must adapt to it, and sometimes this means surrendering things we hold dear, or giving up aspects of ourselves, and perhaps even sacrificing innocents. So when given the chance, we might take flight and try to delink from nature. But this is not possible. We are always already part of nature, and as far as we transcend we will always transcend by transforming within nature and as part of nature, not by eliminating or completely delinking from it. But bourgeois exchange, like Christian ideology, makes us forget this, makes us think we can swindle our way out of our irreducible connection to nature.

It is in this sense that *DE* can claim that bargaining one's way out of sacrifice, by means of self-preserving rationality, is a form of exchange no less than was sacrifice. This ability to bargain creates an identical, enduring self that sacrifices itself by opposing its consciousness to its natural context, and so to speak celebrates itself in its perceived differentiation and uniqueness. Yet it does so without creating harmony. On the contrary, it celebrates in a moment of disharmony. As we see so often in sports, victors sometimes only feels like winners when they have defeated another. More than the positive victory, sometimes the knowledge of the other's defeat may give one the sense of differentiation or feeling of success one craves. So this new self celebrates itself by alienating itself from nature, others, and even aspects of itself in order to survive and to create a stronger, more identical self. But the danger is that this enduring self is a shell of what a human could be, a shadow of what someone really wanted or could have become.

If the victor is essentially as dead as the victim, what exactly is the point of this estrangement? For it is one thing to differentiate but another to alienate. Differentiation itself is not problematic. In fact, it is a necessary condition to form a self. But it is in the how and why that it can become problematic. When the differentiation is purely instrumental, when others are used merely as means, when there is lack of self-reflection, when it is "bourgeois," then differentiation is problematic. In other words, problematic differentiation is un-dialectical differentiation and that is the source of alienation. It is un-dialectical because the loss of consciousness of the intrinsic or higher self destroys the very self that is a product of consciousness. Consciousness is a higher state of being. Self-consciousness is awareness of the present self. When people sacrifice who they are for future self-preservation, they lose that higher self, they lose the self that is more than a vessel for self-preservation. By cutting themselves off from the "consciousness of themselves as nature, all the purposes for which they keep themselves alive—social progress, the heightening of material and intellectual forces, indeed, consciousness itself—become void, and the enthronement of the means as the end."(43) Mastery of self, on which the modern self is founded, involves the annihilation of the subject in whose service that mastery is maintained, because the substance which is mastered "by self-preservation is nothing other than the living entity, of which the achievements of self-preservation can only be defined as functions." (43)

This odyssey, of the Odyssean bourgeois subject, extends to the present insofar as capitalism attempts to satisfy needs, of "the living entity," but since it is determined by domination it "makes the satisfaction of needs impossible and tends toward the extermination of humanity." (43) Whether it is praying to a non-existent god, surrendering an innocent, preventing your best self from emerging, stifling the present, denying one's embeddedness in nature, conning consumers into purchasing useless products, convincing oneself that a Laker victory will bring you happiness, etc., the fact of domination remains while only the victims change. This is why DE can call The Odyssey "one of the earliest representative documents of bourgeois Western civilization." (xviii) The structure of cunning that grows out of myth, continues to the present and in this way the "history of civilization is the history of the introversion of sacrifice." (43) And as said above, the introversion of sacrifice, the ability to renounce the potentially differentiated and still harmonious self continues until those "who renounce give away more of their life than is given back to them, more than the life they preserve." (43)

But to a certain extent it's a catch-22. For if we did not sacrifice or renounce the self "but immediately seized the undiminished whole," (43) we would lose everything, including our life. Sometimes it is not possible to live in the present, not possible to seize the dialectical human meanings available at the time. Sometimes repression is a good thing. But this sort of sacrifice should only be made in pure struggles for survival, in cases where our lives really are at stake, or at opportune moments of history and individual circumstance. It should not be the preferred manner of being-in-the-world; it should not be a constant or normalized. A "forced choice," to use the Lacanian term, should be the exception, and we should be aware of what it means and what we are giving up. This way we can rationally deal with it, accept it or reject it, and get back what we lost when it's appropriate to do so. If it's your money or your life, then perhaps you give up your money. But if it's your meaningful self, your integrity, your genuine being, or the moment that you could seize your humanness and happiness versus your life, then perhaps you don't give priority to self-preservation. Some things should be worth dying for. Socrates said that "the most important thing is not life, but the good life."[1] In any case, the point is forced choices should be extremely rare and only arise in moments of scarcity. When individuals are regularly forced into choosing between unpalatable options and stifling or suppressing human values, one must ask why. When the choice is consistently between dominating and being dominated, then something has gone terribly wrong. What has gone wrong is society itself; society has become a "wrong society" (43) as civilization has been transposed into barbarism.

And the history of wrong society, disguised as enlightenment progress, is a history of power culminating in global capitalism and a modern world filled with vacuous, self-preserving selves dreaming about a world of zombies while not recognizing they already are the walking dead.

Zombies

In the world of the walking dead, power is enlightenment. In a world that abandons human subjectivity for power, instead of power leading away from myth it now dialectically leads back to it. DE reads the myth of the Sirens to illustrate this.(24-27) The Sirens represent the allurement of losing oneself in the past, the past before the sacrifice of a differentiated and yet harmonious self. But at this point in the story Odysseus has suffered much. Over a decade of struggle, from a war he wanted nothing to do with, to a journey home full of twists and turns, created a hero that is hard and cynical now. After all this, the epic hero cannot face the past as a living past but only as something to be used instrumentally, used for his future survival. As Odysseus describes it, he must sail past the Sirens, or at least he insists to his men that he must. Of course one can ask why not take another route? Maybe

---

1 Plato, "Crito" in *The Trail and Death of Socrates* (Indianapolis: Hackett Publishing, 2000) 48.

the winds won't allow for it or maybe the Sirens are too tempting. Maybe Odysseus wants a story to tell; perhaps he wants to make himself a greater hero. It's unclear, but nonetheless we can see that the Sirens represent the struggle between self-preservation and self-annihilation within all of us. Perhaps they represent the secret Kafkaesque yearning of the metaphysical urge, the urge toward death. In any case, what is clear is that the Sirens are seductive and enchant with a promise of happiness and beauty in unsublimated form, but with the underlying understanding that the price for this sublime moment is death.

But Odysseus trusts in his human enlightenment power, and thinks he is going to lose himself in the Siren's song and, at the same time, by having himself tied to the mast, ensure his own preservation. He thinks he has found a loophole around the forced choice of: listen freely but die, or don't listen at all. For his crew, he chooses to deny them all of the pleasure. And he lies to them, telling them that Circe said he must listen. To the crew he acts like it's a punishment, but to himself he keeps the truth of his temptation. Thus his men are told only of the dangers of beauty, and that their ears must be plugged with wax, so they hear nothing. Odysseus orders them to keep rowing no matter what he might say or do. By giving his men the power to ignore his pleas, he is allowing them to, for a moment, play the role of the leader or the dominator. But they must never get a taste of beauty.

As it turns out, getting only a taste may be worse than not hearing a thing. For Odysseus cons himself more so than he cons his crew. When he realizes that he is cheated from uninhibited beauty and happiness, because he has rendered himself impotent by being tied to the mast, it is too late. He must suffer through the song rather than letting it fully embrace him. And he will spend the rest of his days missing what he didn't get to completely experience. He couldn't lose himself in the moment because he was too busy trying to get the crew to untie him, trying to untie himself, trying to hold on to the self that was sailing away from him as quickly as his ship was passing by the island. And as we can imagine the Sirens crushing themselves on the rocks, since their aura was demystified, we can imagine Odysseus's harmonious and differentiated good self smashing against the rocks and taking humanity's reconciliation with it.

Opportunity lost sometimes hurts more than lack of opportunity. The possibility of any reconciliation between happiness and self-preservation, beauty and labor, finding meaning and acting rationally, as well as individual and community, dissolve—and they dissolve because of Odysseus's actions themselves. With Odysseus we see that while enlightened thought may have once freed us from natures' chains, we replaced the chains with stronger, more enduring chains and locked them on ourselves. Rather than confront this truth, Odysseus brags about his adventure without having fully experienced the adventure. Like a Lakers fan at Staples Center, Odysseus cannot experience the world without texting or tweeting about it, without thinking that gods are helping him or gods are impeding him; he cannot experience his life outside the myopic lens of the supernatural and the popular. Like going to Disney World, with its mythic characters and fake adventures, everybody pretends to be having fun because they are supposed to. Although the long lines are a nightmare and the prices are ridiculous, everybody loves Disney. And keep telling yourself that, for before you know it this fake adventure is your life and society's fate. Telling tales can lead one down a path that no one would believe, except that it happened. Do you think the charlatans who concocted a fairy tale about the son of God rising from the dead ever thought that thousands of years later people would still be expecting his return any day, and others would honor the event by dyeing eggs and sitting on the lap of a giant bunny at the mall? Beneath these absurdities, the Odyssean mode of being and worldview sets the structure and limits of modernity and perpetuates the myth of only two options, of life as a forced choice: work with no beauty or try to experience beauty while impotent. His legacy endures.

The legacy of Odysseus is a legacy in which myth and enlightenment take turns tying us to some mast. Enlightenment ensures that we will be alienated from ourselves, others, and the world, and if we push back we simply fall back to a mythic, childlike, and fake reconciliation. So the wise hero takes his social chains like a man, and like Odysseus, "just wriggles through—that is his survival, and all the renown he gains in his own and others' eyes merely confirms that the honor of heroism is won only by the humbling of the urge to attain entire, universal, undivided happiness." (45)

The legacy is confirmed all the way down to identity and its intertwinement with language. Odysseus knows the power of words. When Odysseus saves himself from the Cyclops by telling him his name is "Nobody," he understands that the Cyclops still uses language tautologically, and so can be easily manipulated. Calling himself nobody, like a magic trick for children, can transfer him into nobody for the Cyclops. But Odysseus cannot outwit the dialectic as he regrets this cunning move and tries to correct it. In an act of existential angst that screams "I am somebody!" he yells out his name correctly to the Cyclops as he escapes to his ship. Yet he almost destroys himself and the rest of his crew in this action. He cannot leave without letting Polyphemus know he isn't a "nobody." He mocks Polyphemus as he escapes and asserts his identity again. Not only does it almost do him in, but it also causes future problems for him from Poseidon. As the father of Polyphemus, Poseidon must make Odysseus pay for the attack on his son.

The punishment comes hard and fast after Odysseus leaves Calypso's island and continues even until after the epic ends. Even after reclaiming his home Odysseus must make one more journey for the god. We always have one more journey in the name of God.

The dialectic of enlightenment, as a history of sacrifice and renunciation, is captured in the ambiguity that Odysseus senses but cannot resolve. Odysseus's lack of ability to transcend this contradiction within identity itself lives within us all. This is captured when Horkheimer and Adorno say: In his "self-assertion, as in the entire epic, as in all civilization, is self-repudiation." (53) By calling himself nobody he makes us all nobody. For who can be themselves in a society that is predicated on conning each other? Who can avoid domination in a world that uses language, culture, media, education, government, and industry to manufacture wants and desires? From every corner of our mythic–consumerist society we are served the wine Odysseus seduces Polyphemus with, until everyone is so drunk that it easy to stick a hot poker in our eye and blind us.

Ultimately, though, Odysseus could not experience reconciliation with nature or express human meaning—not because he was alienated from the Sirens or the Cyclops, for these creatures do not and have never existed. Religion, as Marx knew so well, is merely a symptom, not a cause. And like all that is supernatural, the Sirens and Cyclops are products of the human. Against these made-up obstacles, Odysseus's journey home was always already and only linked to the other subjects, to nature, and to the many aspects of himself. Odysseus's problem was, therefore, that he separated himself from his crew and treated them as mere objects. He regarded nature and the past only as a tool, and he was alienated from higher aspects of himself. Finally, he did not recognize his fate as intertwined with all others'. But that is exactly why this text still speaks to us.

Bill and Hillary

Our fates our intertwined because our actions affect others and help define where the future will begin. Odysseus's choices, then, spills into intersubjective things like love. Bourgeois sacrifice has a patriarchal and, as we have seen, a perverted element. In a perverted bourgeois world, relations between others contain perversion. In a perverted bourgeois world, not only must one sacrifice, but one insists that others sacrifice also. If I must give up something dear, then you must too; if I am going to take a risk, so shall you; if I can't have love, then neither shall you; if I was conned, then I will con somebody. In a world like this, people prove they are somebody either by dominating or by allowing themselves to be dominated. If perversion, fraud, deprivation, and betrayal are essential to bourgeois patriarchal relationships, then within Odysseus's journey we can see this by looking at the women who form a central part of his odyssey.

The cliché tells us that behind any successful man there is a woman. Odysseus and Penelope, like Bill and Hillary Clinton, have a complicated relationship. They are intellectual equals and share a bond that is deeper than it may initially seem. Still, as an unrealized self, Odysseus lets other women prevent him from achieving and actualizing true love. Penelope is not enough, Odysseus needs more, and this more starts with Athena. Without Athena, Odysseus doesn't survive or get home. Athena is that best friend that Odysseus can always count on. They both have their own lives, but Athena is always looking out for Odysseus. Like a big sister, she makes sure he is safe, she gives great advice, and she loves him. But the fact that Athena is an immortal goddess limits their mutual understanding[1], and the affection they feel for each other falls short of human friendship and love, and distracts from Odysseus's potential for human friendship and love. Each of us has only so much to give and only a finite amount of time for others. His relationship with Athena serves as a warning for those who become best friends with someone supernatural, someone with a fundamentally different life, or someone whom they do not love.

Odysseus's encounter with Circe, though, hints at the possibilities of human love and touches on the mythic origin of love. Circe represents a time before enlightenment, a "stage of actual magic." (54) Magic here disintegrates the "self which falls back into its power and thus into the form of an earlier biological species." (54) Love, as a kind of magic, dissolves the self into that of another without killing the living entity. The power that dissolves the self, like the feeling of being in love, is a kind of oblivion. When in love time means nothing. Caught in the moment, one can do without food, drink, sleep, or anything else in the world. Love is magic, but it's not a trick. Love is a beautiful contradiction full of risk. It's a place where you must give yourself to another as that person gives himself or herself to you[2]. . . all the while trusting that the other won't sacrifice this self being offered up. For this self being offered up is the only self capable of deep human love, of keeping its differentiation while falling harmoniously into the other. But the contradiction exists because it is a type of magic that allows one to sacrifice for and to another while also keeping one's self. To love is to connect to another as this other connects to you, it is to experience each other as unique individuals, and sorting out exactly what this means is part of the beauty

---

1 This is no small thing. Athena can't figure out why Odysseus is angry that it took her seven years to help him get off Calypso's island. Living in immortal time, she thinks that's rather quick.
2 Alexander Nehamas, *Only a Promise of Happiness* (Princeton: Princeton University Press, 2007).

and danger of love. Love transcends time and yet needs time to give it form. Love may strike instantly, but it takes being together and experiencing life together to unify, solidify, root, and grow all that beauty and desire. But this type of love, a love before bourgeois time, cannot withstand an encounter with the first bourgeoisie.

Circe's magic works on Odysseus's men. His men fall for Circe but she doesn't fall for them. Still, her "primitive," magical self is empathetic and nonviolent. As the men abandon themselves to instinct, to a time before the differentiated self, Circe is able to take them out of their human selves and literally turn them into another species. She denies them her love but keeps them open to the possibility of love. Men who encounter Circe generally get turned into wild creatures like lions and wolves, but with a domesticated aura. Love is a product of civilization but has a pre-civilized frenzy to it, and Circe's man-animals hold this tension in limbo. These men exist the way memories of early unsuccessful attempts at love rest in us, as memories of something human and not human at the same time. Surrounded by these sort-of-men, surrounded by love-lost memories, Circe is waiting for her chance at love. It comes in the form of Odysseus. But as is often the case, Odysseus is too late. Odysseus has already renounced his reconciled, loving self for self-preservation. When Circe recognizes that he can resist her magic, the dialectic pushes them into a bourgeois relationship. In a bourgeois world, Circe's magical self makes Circe as vulnerable as she is ambiguous. Enlightenment, since it cannot stand ambiguity, goes in for premature reconciliation and defines her by bourgeois categories. She becomes the prototypical courtesan who can be a "corrupter and helper" (54) but nothing more.

We are back to a forced choice, now applied to love, in our enlightened world. The ambiguity of Circe, the ambiguity of a hetaera type in civilization, pushes and pulls on love. The hetaera both confers "joy and destroys the autonomy of its recipient." (55) But unlike in the age of enlightenment, Circe does not seek to completely destroy the "Other"; rather, as stated above, she turns her guests into wild beasts that are peaceful. She will pay a price for her lack of hardness, for her ambiguity, for even hinting that liberation comes in not suppressing instinct, for even hinting that a pre-enlightenment stance can be liberating, for showing that for men what "is revoked by their relapse into myth is myth itself." (55) The "violent magic which recalls them to an idealized prehistory not only makes them animals but brings about, in however delusive a form, a semblance of reconciliation." (55) This flight is too much for an enlightened Odysseus to accept and he cannot be tempted by this sort of love, for he is too hard, too "modern," and will use her romanticism against her. Odysseus's misreading of Circe is patriarchal society's misreading of love. By choosing the enlightenment Circe, rather than the magical Circe, Odysseus loses for modernity a tender love unafraid to surrender power.

Odysseus turns Circe into a female bourgeoisie. She becomes "an enigma of irresistibility and powerlessness. Thus she reflects back the vain lie of power, which substitutes the mastery over nature for reconciliation with it." (56) In this relationship, then, Odysseus sleeps with Circe while he resists her magic, and in so doing reduces the relationship to bourgeois contract. In fact, his resistance and coldness, his ability to control his instinct and desire, is what makes him successful. Circe must bow to Odysseus's commands and must turn Odysseus's men back into men in order to end Odysseus's moping about. And with his demands he establishes a patriarchal order. With the turning back of his men into men, he rids the powerful world of a love that goes deeper than the modern self and industrial time can process. Odysseus also, as the more cunning magician, turns Circe into a bourgeois woman who now submits to the man who has resisted her, "the master, the self." (56)

In a world that worships masters, love is not exchanged for love, for the bourgeois species could not care less about use value. So it is no surprise that it is only by first turning desire into a bourgeois contract, by showing he can resist, that Odysseus gains access to Circe's bed. For if Odysseus were to love her unconditionally, he would show he was not master of himself, and that's "reason enough to deny him fulfillment." (57) One must not bring out the good self; rather one must be a cunning bad boy to find love today. The cunning of the dialectic, though, in the end, creates a civilization that breeds loneliness, even and perhaps especially within modern love. The cunning man is able to enslave Circe because, in his refusal to submit to her, he has renounced the self capable of love. Love becomes a game. It's not about giving oneself and letting another give back; rather it's a contract full of lies, loopholes, and bragging rights. Odysseus tells everybody about his encounters with various goddesses, including bragging to his wife. His Facebook page has no privacy features, as love has been reduced to exchange value.

Enlightened love, then, only serves self-preservation. With this reduction of love, all Odysseus's relationships look very similar. "Harlot and wife are complementary forms of female self-alienation in the patriarchal world." (57-8) In a patriarchal world a wife helps one structure family life and brings property to the forefront, while the harlot provides pleasure and leisure. But looking more closely at the wife, she, "like a harlot, mistrustfully scrutinizes the returning Odysseus." (58) Penelope and Odysseus play a perverted game, a type of Hegelian master/slave dialectic, with each other when he returns home. In one intriguing example, Penelope taunts Odysseus by untruthfully telling him she has moved their marriage bed. She hits directly on the lynch pin of bourgeois marriage, the one big taboo. A wife must never cheat on her husband, must never mess with the conjugal bed. Everything else is permitted. She knows that only Odysseus knows that their bed doesn't move, for he built it out of, and around, an olive tree. If she moved the bed, it would be an act of destruction, an uprooting of their whole marriage. It would be an affront to their relationship and his identity. Odysseus built that bed, and like today's hipsters, Odysseus takes his hobbies seriously; nobody better mess with his handiwork or his woman.

Despite the flaws in Penelope's and Odysseus's relationship, we can read their bourgeois marriage as script and see that it nonetheless holds on to a reconciled beauty, even if only implicitly. It hints at Hegel's final stage of history, at differentiation and harmony. It moves beyond the master/slave dialectic and toward mutual recognition, respect, and love. Their first night back together in bed is a magical and beautiful moment that makes us admire and respect Penelope and Odysseus. For despite the complications of marriage, and its history of domination, the concept of marriage still offers something deeper than any individual could attain alone. Penelope speaks the truth when she says that, for this reason, the gods make spouses suffer: for marriage confirms the concept of permanence and the gods are envious of "the happiness guaranteed only by marriage." (58) Marriage not only represents "the account-balancing order of the living but also solidarity and steadfastness in face of death. In it reconciliation grows up around subjugation." (59) So although "marriage forms part of the primal rock of myth at the base of civilization...its mythic solidity and permanence jut from myth" (59) as marriage holds the hope and the promise of true happiness and reconciliation.[1] This sort of love, true love, holds the dialectic of the intrinsic and instrumental in artful balance.

Odysseus's and Penelope's love hints at something deeper than the given, and we can begin to see the positive side of enlightenment when we contrast Penelope with Calypso. Calypso offers a different type of love. She really does love Odysseus, but they just are not right for each other. Their relationship is one of beauty, but it is ironically fleeting on her eternal island. On her island for years, outside of time, they know of no one or anything outside of themselves. One gets the picture of Aristophanes' two halves thinking

---

1 Scalia's dissent in *Obergefell v. Hodges* gets this perfectly backwards. In claiming that "Freedom of Intimacy is abridged rather than expanded by marriage," Scalia conceives of "intimacy" as a quantitative good, an instrumental goal. Against this, human beings realize that intimacy is an intertwinement with another that only increases as you go deeper into each other. That's why marriage equality is so centrally important. It's very difficult to go deeply into intimacy unless your social and political world allows, and in fact encourages, it. Scalia's "fragment" explains much of his regressive world view; it illuminates his desire to be a master.

they found each other and so needing nothing else. No food, just a little ambrosia. History, responsibility, and time do not matter for seven years. Yet the seven year itch comes. And, of course, like a honeymoon, this cannot last, and does not get to the reality of human relationships. Odysseus has a past he cannot ignore, goals to accomplish; and the clock is ticking. Calypso cannot relate to any of this. So he weeps and must get off the island. And Calypso will never understand because Odysseus's life is a human life and gods could never understand or truly comprehend. Leaving Calypso's island, giving up a beautiful body, immortality, pleasure, leisure, comfort, and rest are necessary if one is to be more than a vessel of self-preservation. For these things do not represent true happiness or reconciliation. At best, some are means, but mostly they are distractions. So Odysseus, although ideologically driven, gets that part right...eventually.

It is not just the gods who could never understand the beauty of marriage. Many people today still miss out on love and internalize our vulgar bourgeois legacy. Donald Sterling, although married for nearly sixty years, seems to have missed the happiness of marriage. Rather than cultivating a marriage of depth and love, his time apparently was spent drinking and running around with floozies. Now 80 years old, he's estranged from his wife and on the verge of divorce. Still, he doesn't get it. A few years back, at a party to celebrate the Clippers' making the playoffs, Sterling publically asked the star point guard, Chris Paul, why he was married, given "all the beautiful women in L.A."[1] Paul responded almost like Cordelia in *King Lear*, trapped between a father corrupted by power and two private property seeking sisters, she said: "Love and be silent."[2] Paul simply said: "Because I love my wife." Paul, like Cordelia, seemed to recognize there was no point in explaining to someone like Sterling. But it's not just the vulgar that don't get it. Those who are too spiritually inclined neglect human love or distort it. Like Tim Tebow, they waste their youth on a silly myth; loving a nonexistent guy, they miss out on the beauty and physicality that only the enlightened young can experience. Real love is harder than hanging with party girls or imagining how much Jesus loves you. So despite Odysseus's shortcomings, his marriage and devotion to Penelope is splendid.

While on Calypso's island perhaps Odysseus came to understand that a meaningful human life requires connecting with real people, challenging death's gaze, and feeling at home in one's world. Calypso offered Odysseus a seemingly irresistible deal. Stay with her on her island and he would be forever content and immortal. Despite his desire for self-preservation, despite that for a time she seemed right for him, in the end he realized that he needed

---

1 http://espn.go.com/nba/story/_/id/11105717/sad-last-chapter-donald-sterling-life
2 Shakespeare. *King Lear*. Scene 1.

to leave and get back to Penelope. Odysseus could not realize his human self on Calypso's island and only regained his humanity when he left. Taking chances in life, tasting ambiguity, accepting contingency, not just feeling safe, is part of what it means to be human. Still no one should fault Odysseus for considering a life with Calypso; the attraction is understandable. We all have moments when we dream of immortality and a life without struggle. But upon reflection, we see it does not add up to a human life. Odysseus saw that the only route to human reconciliation and meaning was to make a plan, build a raft, and explicitly assert the authorship of his life. But to get home sometimes you have to go to hell and back first.

Hades is for Real

The farthest point of Odysseus's journey was Hades and an encounter with another woman, this time his mother. He sees the image of his mother but she is "powerless, blind, and speechless" like "when language gives way to images." (59) When language gives way to images, human life has ended. Still these images haunt us, like the past, and form part of human hell. Our unarticulated past is partly a lost past, a past not enriched with linguistic memories, and so cannot be spoken or completely understood. It's dangerous to lose the articulation of the past, as the past is the only path we have encountered. To grasp the past as a human past is to treat it as a living past. But to treat it as living is to come to terms with the blood spilt, and so: "Sacrificial blood is required as pledge of living memory before the shades can speak." (59) When the shades speak, when the truth of the past is articulated, the spell of myth is demystified. "Only when subjectivity masters itself by recognizing the nullity of images does it begin to share the hope which images vainly promise." (59) Human subjectivity recognizes that images are not enough. For the true essence of images "as shades in the world of the dead" (59) are illusions, yet seductive ones. Odysseus's visit to Hades ironically provokes the knowledge that this life is the only life. We must achieve reconciliation in the here and now, with others, and within ourselves. Those in Hades, like those in heaven and hell, can do nothing, for they are nothing.

The trip to Hades reaffirms Odysseus's subjectivity, yet it also foreshadows his unfortunate future. In this way, the trip to Hades links with the end of the epic and Odysseus's mission to wander even further than Hades to sacrifice for Poseidon. He discovers that he must go so far that a stranger will refer to his oar as a fan. He must travel back to the absurd for he has chosen the busybody life of the bourgeoisie. In the place of death, in Hades, he discovers that the only way to have reconciliation with the mythic world is through a joke. Really, who could mistake an oar for a fan? Who could mistake the sky for a vault? Religion is a joke, but the punch line is not funny. The laughter that Poseidon would surely experience from an oar being mistaken for a fan softens the punch line of life. Life ends in death, but perhaps by getting the god to laugh there is hope that his anger will disperse and death will not be so bad. Making a god laugh is metaphor for having good fortune in life. And death will not be so bad if one can have good fortune, if one can seize their human subjectivity, experience tender love, and then, perhaps, laugh at the rest.

For laughter, as part of the dialectic of enlightenment, has a mythic origin which "up to now has been a sign of violence," (60) and yet it also contains its opposite so that perhaps through laughter violence might become aware of itself. Laughter is too often an excuse to not reflect, to be mean, but on occasion, the right laughter can awaken and provoke reflection. In today's world it is the comics and satirists that provoke the deepest reflection in us. Those like Jon Stewart, Joe Rogan, Stephen Colbert, and Ricky Gervais come to mind. Reflection provoked by laughter has the power to reveal what myth could not, that "abolishing death, is the innermost cell of all antimythological thought." (60) Anti-mythological thought is therefore anti-metaphysical thought. Within the deepest myths, in hell or hades no less, we can transcend myth. When we laugh at these silly myths, our "Laughter is in league with the guilt of subjectivity, but... also points beyond that complicity. It promises a passage to the homeland. It is a yearning for the homeland which sets in motion the adventures by which subjectivity, the prehistory of which is narrated in the *Odyssey*, escapes the primeval world." (60) Escaping myth, by yearning for the homeland— call it the homeland urge, is the human way of escaping death.

But it's not always exciting to contemplate this type of escape, this homeland that does not grant the individual subject's immorality. Of course it's more fun and comforting to stay in the realm of the mythic and the metaphysical. The middle chapters of Homer's great epic are clearly the most exciting and memorable.[1] These are the chapters of the great wanderings, of fantasy, magic, goddesses, and monsters. Still, these fetishized adventures are meant for children and obscure the significance of Odysseus's journey and the truth of the world he is a central part of. For his world is a patriarchal, monarchial, religious, and slave-owning world. It is a bourgeois anti-modern world too similar to our own. It is a world where Odysseus's "lordly renunciation, as a struggle with myth, is representative of a society which no longer needs renunciation and domination." (43) But being a lord, he cannot admit this. In the same way that the endless striving for profit sacrifices the present for the never-coming capitalist utopia, the endless struggle with

---

1 Especially Ch. 9

mythic forces sacrifices human beings and human meaning for the never-existent afterlife. Odysseus struggles against myth because he is not at home with himself, others, or the world. His mythic adventures are ideological cover for the loss of his men, his long absence, and his sexual encounters. Odysseus spent two decades away from home for a war of choice, he returned home without any of his men or 24 ships, he missed his son's childhood and adolescence, and he abandoned his wife to fend for herself. His struggles are struggles brought on by unnecessary war, by class struggle, by selfishness, by lack of reconciliation. Like Odysseus how many of our sacrifices are for our myths, our appetites, our military mentality, our economic greed, and our vulgar preservation? What is homeland defense really about?

The paradox of love is connected to the paradox of homeland in the *Odyssey*. Both love and homeland are embedded in myth and have an exchange component, yet at the same time are opposed to myth and to exchange value. Individuals, if fortunate, give way to love; they find tender, human love. It is the same with homeland. Homeland is not an origin to return to; rather it is a future destination that, if fortunate, a people can arrive at. Just as love is not a reunion with one's lost half, as Aristophanes so eloquently suggested, homeland is not a reunion with the lost Garden of Eden. Rather, "nomadism gave way to settlement, the precondition of any homeland." (60) Fixed property, "implicit in settlement is the source of human alienation," and as such homeland must "be wrested from myth." (60-61) Homeland is a state of having escaped origins, to a future with a promise of happiness and with the hope of reconciliation. If Odysseus is going to have reconciliation, it is not enough to get home; he must also unleash it from myth. Like Brody in the television show *Homeland*, caught between conflicting myths, barbaric al-Qaeda terrorist or imperialist American Hawk, Brody's homeland can only come as a future destination. He must escape violent mythic radical Islam and militaristic capitalist America if he is to get home. But like Odysseus's maidservants, it's not so easy when you don't have power. The maidservants' fate is Brody's fate.

Of course wily Odysseus doesn't end up like Brody. Odysseus gets home but he doesn't escape myth or exchange value. Odysseus preserves himself but changes nothing. He slaughters many of the children of his friends, he hangs many of his servants, and before we know it he is about to go off on another adventure, away from home in the service of the gods. So what has Odysseus gained with this new self unable to stay put, and unwilling to enjoy and get to know the son whose childhood he missed, and incapable of staying with his patient wife who was so willing to hold the household together in his absence? Is this all we can say about Odysseus's return — that at least he didn't get hanged?

DE's reading of the *Odyssey* is a lesson in dialectical philosophy, of reading false yet fruitful representations of truth. Rather than singing and mindlessly celebrating the Homeric epic, *DE* slows it down so as not to be seduced by the false longing for a lost original state. When given pause we can begin to picture homeland as an escape from myth, as a promise of reconciliation. By slowing the epic down we ourselves can journey from lost original state to homeland. A reflective slow reading transposes epic into novel, and as novel truth begins to emerge. Reading the *Odyssey* as a novel "does not falsify myth so much as drag it into the sphere of time, exposing the abyss which separates it from homeland and reconciliation." (61) But it is not just myth that is far from a human homeland and reconciliation. It is enlightenment itself that through the dialectic is still searching for its promised land, its homeland; and like Odysseus has taken many excursions.

Although we like to think that rationality has elevated civilization out of barbarism, it's really not that simple. For civilization, as the 20th century proved all too well, has been as barbaric as the primeval world. But through self-reflection, through novel-like reading of ourselves, violence may be forced to pause. "Speech itself, language as opposed to mythical song, the possibility of holding fast the past atrocity through memory" (61) is an important value of a novelistic reading of the Homeric tale. As epic, the Homeric song aestheticizes the horrors with glory and honor, Kleos and Time, and gives it all a feeling of fate or inevitability. But when speech pauses, when we slow down and reflect, this "allows the events narrated to be transformed into something long past, and causes to flash up a semblance of freedom that civilization has been unable wholly to extinguish ever since." (61)

There is a horrible scene toward the end of the *Odyssey*. After Odysseus, his son, and a few others kill all the suitors, they don't stop there. For them justice entails punishing those who, most likely under duress, conceded to the suitors. The maidservants are forced to clean up and dispose of the bodies of the suitors they fed and slept with. Then Odysseus and his son hang all of the maidservants. In verse this passes quickly and is "expressionlessly compared to the death of birds in a trap." (61) Homer then reports that "For a little while their feet kicked out, but not for very long." (60) This "not for very long," as paused out in prose, stops the narrative and "keeps a record, as in a novel, of the twitching of the subjugated women." (61) The report, now as written, mediated, and considered, rather than merely heard, immediate, and sung, prevents us "from forgetting the victims of the execution and lays bare the unspeakably endless torment of the single second in which the maids fought against death." (62) If we can hold onto this report, not for instrumental use but as part of our lived past to be redeemed, we can begin to have hope. For as part of our lived past, "hope lies in the fact that it is long past." (62) By putting it in time, reporting the deed, reflecting on it, and acknowledging the horror and injustice, the promise of the tender and good self sustains.

Still, memory alone doesn't conquer all, and the thin line connecting "prehistory, barbarism, and culture" (62) remains. Modernity with its enlightenment reason feigns control of that line and so becomes mythic even as it rejects myth as this "reason that represses mimesis is not merely its opposite. It is itself mimesis: of death." (44) In other words, the logic is the same, and as such it carries self-annihilation as much as self-preservation within it. It mimics human death as death is the end of subjectivity. The end of human subjectivity can come not only from literally dying but from the sacrifice of the self. The creation of sly individuals attests to this. The sarcastic phrase: "Wow, you're acting like a decent person today" captures it while also legitimating the untruth of guile. Sarcasm is an adaptive mechanism in the face of greater strength, it signals death, while it also holds the memory of something different. But when deceptive guile "becomes an element of character" (43), the product of self-preservation regresses from novel back to epic, into the urge toward death, and without reflection it becomes an imitation without understanding. "Imitation enters the service of power when even the human being becomes an anthropomorphism for human beings." (45) When humans have become "an anthropomorphism for human beings," when civilization mimics death, then we have the death of civilization.

Epic Fail

With the death of civilization, perhaps we are back in the age of the Epic. Homer's epic celebrates Odysseus because of his cunning, his success, and his seemingly self-conscious adherence to his way of life. Odysseus, perhaps, made an existential choice, and was unapologetic about it. But this Odyssean self has been internalized by the Western mind as "the human being becomes an anthropomorphism for human beings." Instrumental reason, and its moment of fraud, has become totalitarian; it is the standard mode of operation today. It has become mythic and poetic and is sung unreflectively and celebrated instinctively. The Odyssean self-conscious moment has been incorporated into the modern apparatus and into language, so that no one seriously questions our mode of exchange. Every day we hear "I'm just trying to get mine" or "those who snooze, lose" or "I just want to get paid" or "it's not in my job description" or "that's above my pay scale," etc. The Odyssean self is now the rage of the machine. From bankers and investors to athletes and ministers, the idea of conning and cunning, profit and selfishness, is common sense and no longer has to be articulated, defended, or justified. Neither Wall Street nor Kobe Bryant finds their max contracts problematic. Rather, anyone who was to take less would be seen as a fool. The "transcendental subject of knowledge, as the last reminder of subjectivity, is itself seemingly abolished and replaced by the operations of the automatic mechanism of order, which therefore run all the more smoothly" (23) until logic itself is free of thought. This is why *DE*'s suggestion "to laugh at logic when it runs counter to humans"[1] is not problematic. One might think that it is.[2] Habermas[3] and others claim *DE* is abandoning rationality as *DE* pushes back against logic, while in fact the laugher is aimed at an irrational, abstract logic that cannot contemplate concrete human interests. The difference can be seen quickly by comparing G-, the Prefect of Police, and C. Auguste Dupin in Edgar Allan Poe's "The Murders in the Rue Morgue." All one can do is laugh at G-, while contrasting him with Dupin's logic that emphasizes careful observation and slow reading.[4] Like Dupin's method, the *DE* is a critique of a logical system that runs pre-reflectively, naively, affirmatively, and without critical analysis. *DE* is not critiquing rationality in itself. It is actually a proto-defense of a Habermasian type of reason that seeks understanding, insists on human meaning, and values consensus. A logic that tells us to hang maidservants, drop the bomb, approve the Patriot Act, or deny citizens health care may be instrumentally logical but not humanly rational. An outcomes–output–outsourced logic need not demand our respect. *DE* is right; we should laugh at this logic.

As thought gives way to an instrumental system, the question of sacrifice and renunciation takes on a new significance because the loss of self becomes institutionalized and normalized within the system until it is not seen or felt as loss. No one is asking to be unbound. Odysseus lamented what he lost and yearned for it, despite his existential choice. He seemed to understand he was giving something up. He tried to avoid going to the Trojan War in the first place and was angry it took so long to get back home. But the modern consciousness has difficulty even understanding what this lost self is, let alone explicitly longing for it. How many people actually question the way our society is set up? How many people find problematic the notion of working for thirty years with little rest or vacation on the small chance

---

1 I'm using Vogel's translation here. Steven Vogel, *Against Nature* (Albany: State University of New York Press, 1996) 67. For Jephcott's translation, see p. 180 of *DE* (2002).

2 Vogel takes *DE* to task on this point. In fact, for a different interpretation of *DE* than is offered here, one that argues that *DE*'s critique gives priority to the object side of knowledge, check out Vogel's excellent book.

3 Habermas, *The Philosophical Discourse of Modernity* (The MIT Press: Cambridge, 1992) Ch. V.

4 Edgar Allan Poe, *The Annotated Tales of Edgar Allan Poe* (Avenel Books: New York, 1986).

that when they are sixty-five they can retire in Florida for a few years, play some golf, and then die? Has modern civilization created a world where most people have actualized their subjectivity or has it been an epic fail? If it is a fail, then the question is why. Perhaps we are too consumed with consumption and with our myths to answer. Perhaps we are too distracted by things like sports.

In our culture, sports are entertainment. They are meant to give us a break from work and thought. They are a type of escape and a chance to enjoy competition. We root for the sports teams and individuals that we can identify with. Perhaps we root for our local team or follow who our family cheers for. Often, the basis for our support is not clear to us, and sometimes it's irrational. A name, a rumor, a tattoo, or haircut might determine whether we like or dislike an athlete or a team. Politics or religion may color our devotion to a sports organization, and so on.

But as moderns we don't just have to unreflectively mimic the Bard. Although sports are ideological, they can become dialogical and novelesque. In other words we can consciously take control of the meaning sports have in our lives. We don't have to just unreflectively consume. In fact there is something about sports that "naturally" promotes reflection. It seems we cannot help but continually reflect and redefine our loyalty to these games. Over time our interests change and we might pick up a new sport (like World Cup soccer), we might give one up (like the gladiatorial games), and our devotion to various teams and individuals seems always, at least partly, to be based on more than athletic considerations. In this way we can say, sports transcends sport. Sometimes athletics move us into a realm of seeking understanding and truth beyond the value of the sporting event itself. We might reflect and discuss the ethics of boxing, or cage fighting, or concussions in football, the role of genetics, PEDs, etc., and these conversations can lead to reflection about who we are. Sports seem to naturally invoke critical debate and dialogue. Talking about sports gets us talking about who we are and what we are. Turn on any sports talk show and you can hear the games being broken down and analyzed with logical clarity and analytic detail. And the good shows like Inside the NBA, and Max and Marcellus, combine rational analysis with wit, "mythic stories" of athletic feats, and carnivalesque entertainment. And these shows go beyond the games and the athletes to issues of what it means to be human. Sports can and often do become transcendent in a human sort of way. Sports naturally invoke passion, excellence, and commitment from both the participants and spectators as we see elements of our good selves, our better selves, struggling for existence. Sports can push our minds and bodies beyond themselves, and it's really difficult to achieve excellence without a present-centered consciousness. Those who are merely driven by money or glory can't compete with those intrinsically zoned in. In this way we see a human transcendence unfold in real time. The athlete who celebrates too soon gets tackled before the end zone; the basketball player who has not practiced enough misses the free throw and loses the game.

But we must be careful not to let these human games transcend into something beyond us and we must guard against the eclipse of their intrinsic enjoyment. As a business, sports can quickly become too instrumental, and as meaning-giving they can too easily become religion. Everyone recognizes that in our society it is hard for this desire for transcendence to simply stay within the human, to stay intrinsically and instrumentally balanced. It often becomes irrational as people link the games to profit, nationalism, religion, and even identity. Sports can become tribal rather quickly. Religion today can quickly link to any sport or activity because religion has become de-centered in the modern world. Žižek hits on this point when he says: "religion is no longer fully integrated into and identified with a particular cultural life-form, but acquires autonomy, so that it can survive as the same religion in different cultures."[1] Religion seems to survive and in fact thrive in sports culture.

As sports have gained metaphysical status, we might say modernity has become Tebowesque. This is a sign we have become nihilistic and are hiding the nihilism from ourselves. When kids play sports, it's for fun; they just play the game, hang out with each other, and compete. It's intrinsically meaningful and instrumentally valuable. When people (usually adults) link religion to sports, it exposes their emptiness and reveals something vacuous about modern life and religion. For we all rationally know that it is absurd to bring religion into sports, but at the same time religion is deep into sports. With priests and ministers in the locker rooms, constant individual prayer during games, and group worship after the game, religion justifies and grounds a meaningless modernity. By making sports metaphysical it corrupts sports and prevents the modern world from seeing when it has succumbed to nihilism. Watching Stephen Curry's mother train his young daughter to point to the heavens when Steph makes a three pointer makes it impossible to ignore the desperate desire to unite the metaphysical with a basketball game. The media's constant attention to Curry's loyal family reeks of consumer manipulation and nihilistic, mythic fear, despite the fact that his shots seem to rain down from heaven. Religion doesn't make sports better, and religion doesn't make people better. Rather, religion steals the good self, the living entity, and reifies it into an otherworldly experience; it makes people believe that God is rooting for their team. As

---

1 Žižek, *The Puppet and the Dwarf* (Cambridge: MIT Press, 2003) 3.

such the intrinsically good self cannot emerge and the strategic, nihilistic world cannot be challenged. Religion protects the vulgar modern world by using the innocent human self for its own fearful and power driven purposes. So we end up having sacrificed a meaningful self for self-preservation, but rather than acknowledging it, we have repackaged it with a metaphysical belief system to outwit ourselves about who and what we are. Today we see that contemporary religion mystifies sports and, holds up, justifies, and rationalizes a nihilistic self while concealing the nihilistic self from consciousness. Hence the potential of modernity is undermined from within and from above.

The reading of *The Odyssey* in DE provides a concrete, although mythical, example of dialectics as determinate negation. Besides reminding us of the intrinsic worth and enjoyment of this wonderful story, it's a rational use of myth to provoke understanding of how we actually carve up the world. How our human needs, wants, fears, and desires are mediated through the world, and how we construct the world through this mediation is revealed. In this way determinate negation holds the materiality of the world together even as it transcends it. And as everything dialectical, this negative transcendence is what it is not and it is not what it is. In other, less Hegelian jargon, Odysseus is us, as we are ancient. Just as the Greeks unreflectively cheered for Odysseus and ignored or justified his brutality, our society unreflectively praises the Christian. Today Christianity is the epic sung throughout our culture. How many times have you heard someone say: "He's a good person, he's a Christian"? If modern, capitalist society has integrated the Christian cunning self into its system, then one can wonder if the modern self suffers the same fate as the Odyssean self. Odysseus outwitted himself, and to be religious in America today might mean that one has outwitted oneself. To be Christian today means to sacrifice the "sacred" self while claiming sacredness. For it really doesn't take deep analysis to know that Jesus would never play pro football, the stock market, go to shopping malls, drive SUVs, or watch Fox news.

So while Horkheimer and Adorno call Odysseus the prototype of the bourgeois individual, we might ask if Odysseus is now the prototype of a Christian Conservative. Odysseus, although always cunning, is consistently holy. He leans on Athena like today's Christian leans on Jesus. She's always close and can be called whenever Odysseus needs something. Religion is used, both by the ancients and moderns, to further success and to feel safe. Yet today, as modern, the Christian is much more instrumentally inclined. Can you imagine Joan of Arc doing a Jockey commercial? Tebow has.

Success today is described with the same overdetermination that occurs in *The Odyssey*. Turn on any sports coverage and every other athlete credits his or her success to something metaphysical, not just the time and effort he or she has put in, and the real people who have helped, but also to God. Odysseus himself always has a strategic and mythic explanation for his success. Likewise, from UFC fighters to aspiring Presidents, a metaphysical calling, religious explanation, and spiritual grounding are as necessary sound bites as the mundane human accounts of one's success, reasoning, and choices. But the metaphysical explanation is never so present or so trustworthy that it trumps the strategic aspects. No sane person simply relies on God. Rather, we all lean heavily on the institutions of modernity: schools, coaches, clubs, and mentors, all the way up to the police, corporations, the military, and the government. If anyone seriously thinks Americans truly believe God will protect us, they must never have seen the United States defense budget. This overdetermination prompts one to further suspect that the metaphysical is really just holding up, justifying, and rationalizing a nihilistic world. Myth and abstract logic work together, capitalism and Christianity work together, to perpetuate an instrumental, valueless world and a cunning lifeless self.

We can further see the price of bourgeois sacrifice and ideology by contrasting the *Odyssey* with the *Iliad*. Self-preservation is not central for Achilles. He goes to war knowing it will end in his death. The metaphysical urge is also not central. Achilles warns Odysseus not to sacrifice a long human life for shallow honor and glory. Unlike Joan of Arc or Achilles, Odysseus is all about survival and success. Likewise, modern Christians are cautious and cunning creatures who enjoy all the spoils of modernity but run to church (actually, they probably drive a Lexus) on Sunday, or says a sincere prayer when they are in a pinch. Religion makes them feel special and ethical, yet it rarely affects their bottom line. Odysseus and the Christian Conservative survive the big waves of the sea and the stock market. Yet ultimately what does not survive is a self with meaningful commitments or interests beyond self-preservation or beyond individual success and instrumental ends. "Good" Christians spend their weekdays exploiting and conniving and enjoying modernity, and on the weekends they purify themselves (and of course watch football). So are these metaphysical beliefs really meaningful, or are they self-rationalizations justifying self-preservation and success? This question has been raised to a societal level for Americans after 9/11. Have we maintained who we are, and are we able to honestly say we are good? Or has our quest for self-preservation required us to do things that have corrupted us, and can we even see the corruption? Would Jesus wage a war on terror? Can a Christian conscience condone drone strikes?

Inferno Justice

Most Americans would be deeply offended to hear that religion is an ally of nihilism. Rather, they would argue that religion guards against nihilism and claim that religion helps keep us moral and provides protection against our "darker" side. Of course there's an abundance of historical evidence to refute that notion. The Western self has been on quite an odyssey and we can read the history of the humanities, not just *The Odyssey*, as a struggle with the notions of sacrifice and renunciation. Still, it really does start with *The Odyssey* and the ambiguity it invokes in us. On the one hand, Odysseus is admirable in his ability to survive, have adventures, outwit gods and humans, and get home to Penelope. On the other hand, we cringe over his callous indifference to losing all his crew, his seven years with Calypso, the murder of the family servants and so on. Christianity seems like a pretty good antidote to much we find distasteful in the ancient world. So at some level it seems that modern religion is supporting an ethical life and protecting us against an individualistic and selfish ideology. This reaches its self-reflective pinnacle in *The Confessions*. Augustine is a hero to many religious people even today. Augustine really did try to cultivate the honest self-reflection necessary for enlightenment. But today few want to spend their lives reading and studying Augustine and the Bible. The Old Testament, in particular, is problematic in its celebration of violence. Further, let's be honest, it's rather boring and so is just not that inspirational a text; most believers just rely on their local minister to feed them the narrative. It's a kind of mimesis. This allows for easy ideological manipulation, and the ethical and meaning-giving justification of Christianity begins to crack. And under that crack the true foundation of religion begins to seep out.

And yet it's clearly a sign of progress that so many want to be inspired by the Bible but really cannot be. The thought of being religious makes people feel good. Most people want to be good and are pretty good. People don't need religion to be good, or to find meaning, or to be inspired, but most just don't recognize they don't need it. Most people find meaning through their families, friendships, jobs, hobbies, and community. Reflect for a moment and you realize that going to a good film or cheering for a deserving sports hero inspires more deeply and connects more meaningfully than archaic religion. Good films and professional sports give us imaginary examples, and living individuals, to help guide our lives. These experiences, added to our family, friends, education, knowledge of human history, and the other concrete people around us, provide plenty of inspiration. You don't also have to believe some dude thousands of years ago walked on water to want to make something out of your life. When we can admit in public that comic book heroes, pagan tales, and existing elite athletes, friends, teachers, loving relatives, and other inspiring individuals in our world are much more moving than the absurd and often sinister (check out Genesis 19) biblical myths, it will signal an advance in humanity. Unlike contemporary religion, myths we admit are myths don't so easily invoke the metaphysical urge. They expand the human imagination without the injunction that the stories are literally true. With these myths we don't have to pretend that the characters and events actually took place sometime ago, and we actually have better, more modern and more relevant models from which to draw inspiration. But if one insists on looking to regular old Christianity for meaning, one must at least admit that God is the ultimate devotee of instrumental reason. Only a parent on an extreme power trip would insist his children follow his rules for life (in God's case, it's even after life). Only a control freak, with no notion of justice or mercy, could punish humans as heartlessly as the Bible or Dante entertains.

In any case, by the time we get to Dante, any decent human being starts to have real trouble explaining the logic of its justice. In the end only a few can rationalize it. If one can con oneself into finding that justice is served in Dante's inferno, it is not a long trip to finding justice in our class society, where large segments of the population exist in a kind of inferno. Rationalizing Dante is good training for rationalizing the ghetto, racism, homophobia, and exploitation of the developing world. We end up with a world of economic conservatives and liberal bureaucrats (with their bodyguards and secret service, perhaps) acting like frat boys while in their 50s and 60s, selling their stocks like indulgences, going to strip clubs, popping Viagra, driving convertibles, and remaking the idea of the last man into the phat man. All brought up in Christian America, yet their ethical and metaphysical upbringing has been exposed. Religion as protector of morality and foundation of intrinsic good has been unmasked. And behind that mask we see the ugly face of greed, cynical economic calculation, and self-preservation at all costs. But the mask is on so tight that most don't see that a Christian Conservative is an oxymoron. Rather like Dante finally realizing that those in hell deserve their punishment, the modern consciousness has finally accepted that Christianity and capitalism is the happy match.

So while the standard line is that Christianity guards against nihilism, we see that Christianity is itself nihilistic. If God exists, then life is meaningless. For if God exists, we must search and twist until everything we witness, experience, and believe, fits into God's plan. If it doesn't fit, then we are not trying hard enough. So against the view that God cultivates intrinsic worth, we see that the self that sacrifices for religion is renouncing the intrinsic good for a God that demands instrumental acceptance to his metaphysics and for his metaphysics.

Today it still takes a big step to see beyond the horizon of the supernatural. But if mythic thought, and modern religion specifically, have a substantial instrumental element it becomes clear that religion cannot protect the good human self. The mask of religion, which initially looks like protection, is really shielding strategic action and protecting nihilism. It's problematic to think that religion can push back against instrumental reason when it is so intertwined with it. Caught in a Christian–capitalist vortex, myth and enlightenment spin in a vicious circle until everywhere it all becomes different layers of Dante's hell, so to speak.

Dante could not see beyond the Christian horizon of paradise, purgatory and hell. Yet if Dante could have looked a little beyond Christianity he would have seen that there are planets beyond Jupiter and no such thing as hell. Likewise, perhaps, we have to look outside capitalism and religion to see there are other human possibilities, and no such need for the metaphysical urge to situate the self. Today getting beyond these fake horizons might be the precondition for seeing our human horizon.

G. K. Chesterton's book *Orthodoxy* explains the horizon of Christianity from a believers' standpoint. For Chesterton, Christianity is the ultimate horizon of human experience. Christianity requires that one accept that the ability to love another person requires the awareness that we love God more because Jesus died for our sins.[1] Besides the fact that this is just creepy, as we saw earlier, it fogs up what human love really is, what it truly means. Chesterton unwittingly is just selling a monotheistic version of bourgeois exchange applied to love. Jesus died for your sins, and you signed the contract via original sin, so now pay up. The fraud exists on many levels but perhaps most egregiously in that, in an act of magic, we are supposed to believe that a supernatural being can die but not really die. It sounds as ridiculous as a Sunday morning infomercial. As Sade's Juliette puts it: "A dead God!" "Nothing is more comical." (76) When you get to re-up, to rise from the dead, it's a fake sacrifice you are making. It's like playing a video game and having multiply lives in which to win. I'll reset the game, I'll pretend to die so I can take credit for saving you, and now you owe me with your life and love. Furthermore I get to decide how and when your life has meaning because of my "sacrifice." Meanwhile the real sacrifice is that humans must renounce their humanity to follow God. The moment of fraud in prayer and sacrifice is now a fraud on civilization.

From the perspective of *DE*, this transcendence of human meaning makes everything meaningless. Chesterton's idea of reconciliation is like singing Homer's *Odyssey*. It sounds beautiful only when it is sung with no pauses, when there is no time to reflect. Go into most churches and you can

---

1 Žižek, *The Puppet and the Dwarf* (Cambridge: MIT Press. 2003) 47.

see the Christian frenzy, the letting go, the primitive mimesis. A conception of meaning (making sense of one's life) and reconciliation (connecting that sense to others) worthy of human beings is vastly different. Meaning and reconciliation worthy of human beings is not concerned with overcoming alienation from God. Rather, human meaning and reconciliation are created by overcoming alienation from nature, others, and the self. It is through and through a human horizon in that a meaningful world is not just mediated through us, but is actually constructed by us. The recognition of this dialectical power is accessible through consciousness and self-reflection. We are always already interpreting the world, and the world's horizon is our horizon, and seeing beyond it is to further construct it and ourselves.

When people recognize that meaning and reconciliation come only from us, this need not lead to despair. Inspiration, responsibility, authorship, and human power can now flow from the recognition of the beauty of our creations. We have the power to make sense of our lives and to connect that sense to our world without killing our living entity, without destroying ourselves. Demystifying our still sacred ancient and modern myths makes them no greater and essentially no different than Marvel comics and Greek mythology. But as demystified, they can be read to expand the human horizon. For despite the vicissitudes of modernity, it has proved we are not simply tied to Odysseus's mast. When we unchain ourselves from the dogmas of religion and capitalism new horizons appear. Yet it is true that we are on a boat that is hard to steer and in an ocean difficult to navigate. One day the ship, our world, will sink and never be seen again. Yet, despite our ultimate fate and despite the waves, we can see that all directions reflect, illuminate, and expand the human horizon. So until we go down, we row.

Chapter 2. The Enlightenment Trap

In the 1944 and 1947 preface to the *DE*, Horkheimer and Adorno make clear where their worry with modernity lies. Their concern is that "the gifts of fortune themselves become elements of misfortune" because "progress is reverting to regression." (xviii) The misfortune, as they see it, is not simply that the culture industry, including things like "the sports palace, are obtusely liquidating metaphysics" but that "these things are themselves becoming metaphysics, an ideological curtain, within the social whole, behind which real doom is gathering." (xviii) This real doom is barbarism disguised as civilization. Fueled by instrumental reason and driven by the march of capitalism, it seeps into every crease and crevice of our lives and is gathering and colonizing our minds and bodies. Civilization transforms into barbarism, yet is so seamless it goes largely unnoticed. Still, there is no escape and no going back because "Myth is already enlightenment, and enlightenment reverts to mythology." (xviii)

Linking the two is fear and specifically fear of the unknown. Myth and enlightenment are both reactions to fear but use different strategies to cope with fear. Myth invents a master to protect the human, while enlightenment promises the human that it can be the master. We will explore these dynamics, but to be true to the dialectic will proceed indirectly and twisted, like the path through myth and enlightenment itself. For *DE* is explicitly a work of "philosophical fragments"[1] and this reading is also fragmented and sectioned in a manner meant to illuminate the text for our age. But the fragmentary nature of the writing, in both cases, stylistically serves to illuminate truth through an aesthetically–philosophical representation of the dialectic.

---

1 "Philosophical Fragments" is the subtitle of *Dialectic of Enlightenment*

Enlightenment refers to both a concept and an historical time. To even talk about enlightenment is to be trapped in the dialectic of enlightenment, since it began long ago and has colonized our language. Still, language is both a trap and a means of emancipation. This dialectic, called enlightenment, which "aimed at liberating human beings from fear and installing them as masters" (1) first flickered in early humans, developed implicitly in myth, gained social consciousness during the Enlightenment Age, and finally became the unconscious motor in the apparatus that is our contemporary world. On this journey, enlightenment, understood "as the advance of thought," (1) became totalitarian, barbaric, and a form of domination.

DE is a pessimistic but consistent text. Our tendency toward barbarism is not just some wrong road taken. Rather it is inherent within enlightenment thinking itself: "the very concept of that thinking, no less than the concrete historical forms, the institutions of society with which it is intertwined, already contains the germ of the regression which is taking place everywhere today." (xvi) Mythic fear prompts ignorance of the dialectical nature of enlightenment and replaces it with a reified conceptual definition. As a congealed concept enlightenment loses its richness and the interpretive moment in conceptual analysis gets forgotten. If the concept of enlightenment itself is problematic, if it contains barbarism within it, then Horkheimer and Adorno are correct to assert that the cause of the regression of enlightenment into mythology is "to be sought not so much in the nationalist, pagan, or other modern mythologies concocted specifically to cause such a relapse as in the fear of truth which petrifies enlightenment itself." (xvi) This fear of truth is a fear of departing from the accepted facts of the current society, and a fear of allowing anything outside society's norms to penetrate the so-called enlightened perspective. It is a fear of being anything but a master.

DE asks us to confront our fear and to face truth and this requires going back to the origin of enlightenment thinking, back to the dialectical origin of the concept. This is why criticism's like those of Richard Wolin completely miss the mark. Wolin says that Horkheimer and Adorno's "strategy of searching for Nazism's origins in the Age of Enlightenment"[1] is not plausible. According to Wolin, "Nazism and the Enlightenment are ideological opposites."[2] Wolin makes a double mistake in confusing the Age of Enlightenment with the concept of enlightenment, and by misunderstanding the dialectical nature of the concept of enlightenment itself. *DE* never asserts that the origin of Nazism is in the Enlightenment Age. *DE* makes a stronger, more radical claim. The origin of Nazism is within the concept of enlightenment. The concept of enlightenment contains barbaric elements and mythic traces

---

1 Richard Wolin, *The Frankfurt School Revisited* (New York: Routledge, 2006) 5.
2 Ibid.

within it. In other words the concept of enlightenment is a product of an unreflective dialectical moment that originated from mythic fear. Nazism and the Enlightenment Age both are connected to this history and are not ideological opposites but rather are intertwined moments of enlightenment reason and mythic fear. Superficially, enlightenment may seem ideologically opposed to Nazism and to myth, but in its DNA enlightenment thinking shares the same deep structure as mythic thought. This deep structure is one that believes in non-human transcendence, in metaphysical truth, in the final solution. Myth and enlightenment are two sides of the same coin: a coin invented by humans to overcome fear, to satisfy the metaphysical urge. This coin promises to buy our way out of fear, to secure us a ticket to the transcendent, by creating a world in its own image, a world with no outside.

The Age of Enlightenment in particular was oblivious to its own metaphysical myth that linked Truth, Goodness, and Beauty. The lack of reflection and misunderstanding of its sublimated mythic fear, not its specific method, is what makes the Enlightenment Age ideologically problematic.[1] The Enlightenment Age, in thinking it had transcended myth, fell victim to its own myth and naively held to Francis Bacon's happy match in which the World would perfectly align with the human mind and human will. In reality the happy match was just a myth, a ploy to alleviate the fear of the unknown. It was a brilliant attempt to satisfy the metaphysical urge but ultimately failed to escape the enlightenment trap.

Dancing with the Metaphysical Stars

But what exactly is the metaphysical urge? According to Raymond Geuss,[2] it is the sense that there must be an essential nature to reality and a feeling that humans have a special place within that reality. The metaphysical is typically interpreted as something that transcends normal experience, or refers to a reality beyond or outside of our empirical world, beyond or outside human interpretation. It is held by many, since at least Plato, that perhaps humans have a metaphysical need to know what is beyond the bounds of our everyday experience and to find a standpoint which is not of this world, a standpoint which will allow us to "see" ultimate reality. From such a standpoint we could, without fear or doubt, know how to live our lives and know what it all means. Insight into this other reality and how our lives fit into it would make the heart calm, make the center hold, and ease the

1 This point is rarely understood even today. Steven Pinker in his latest book, *The Better Angels of our Nature*, repeats the incorrect claim that "Critical Theory" was a straightforward critique of rationality and the Enlightenment Age. See pp. 642-3 for his misreading.
2 Raymond Geuss "On the Usefulness and Uselessness of Religious Illusions" in *Outside Ethics* (Princeton: Princeton University Press, 2005)

uneasiness of knowing that we are simply dancing on a floating ball while hurling through space. By getting behind it all, by seeing what lies behind or beyond appearances, one might find the meaning and reconciliation that would alleviate the fear and make sense of human life.

But clearly the metaphysical urge carries with it assumptions one need not accept today and in fact are hard to accept at this point in history. Assumptions like thinking everyone does or should feel this urge, or that there is an ultimate reality behind appearances, or that humans have a special place in the universe, seem extremely dubious, and the onus is on those who hold these assumptions to justify and prove them. Still, whether true or not, or good or bad, it does seem correct that some sort of metaphysical urge lingers deep within many people and takes various historical forms. A longing for the intrinsic is not hard to understand. It manifests itself in religion as a cure to the problem of meaning, the answer to why be moral, and the ticket to escape death. It grows in the rational and scientific mind that believes its analytical human tools can unlock eternal mysteries of the universe and senses that the human cogito is specially equipped to solve and reveal them. Defined as the Other of instrumental reason, one can see why Horkheimer and Adorno might be, although ambivalently, attracted to it.

Nonetheless one can also see right away that the urge, as traditionally defined, is problematic. Unlike the definition of a triangle, there is not one clear definition or even understanding of the metaphysical urge. But the metaphysical urge, to be satisfied, requires a clear definition, a timeless answer. If it is not timeless and universal, the riddle is not solved and contingencies abound. The metaphysical urge is not supposed to be subject to our whims, to instrumentality, to history or contingencies, in a word: to the human. If the urge can change or if the answer could change, the grounding or centering sought dissolves. If we could wake up tomorrow and the urge has migrated, it scratches somewhere new, then our seemingly absolute religious and metaphysical answers might, and in fact for many have, fallen short and so won't satisfy the itch. Has the itch moved or has it gone away, has it increased or has it been satisfied? Do we have to follow Hume on the problem of induction and forget about it and just go dancing? Actually today those who defend the metaphysical urge also tend to watch shows like *Dancing with the Stars*. If that helps satisfy the sublime urge for something intrinsic, an in-itself, for transcendence, for escape, we have become Nietzsche's last men in a way even more pathetic than he could have imagined.

Perhaps Kafka was closer to the truth when he supposedly said: "The metaphysical urge is only the urge toward death."[1] Another way of putting

---

1 http://notesfromaroom.com/2010/07/27/kafka-quotes-2/

this is that the metaphysical urge is an attempt to escape the human condition with its unavoidable contingent, interpretive, and historical nature. Defining the urge as an urge toward death gives it the existential significance and weight it deserves. The enduring salience of Silenus's pessimistic philosophy spans from the ancient Greeks to today. The desire to have never lived is the ultimate response to the contingencies of being human. Close to that is dying quickly, which ensures you don't have to struggle with nature, make yourself into somebody, or tackle the existential question of what it all means. Although pessimistic, it has a poetic elegance to it. On our darker days most of us would acknowledge that this sort of metaphysical urge is within us. Perhaps that's why, most of the time, we forget the dark meaning of the metaphysical urge. Rather, with rose-colored glasses, we have reinterpreted the metaphysical urge as a hopeful impulse linking us to something greater out there. But as the explorers found out in that bad film *Prometheus*, what's out there might not make our hearts calm. Like the forgotten human roots of myth, we have forgotten that the urge signals a sinister truth. The metaphysical urge may be, like an alien baby, inside us and it may be something we need to kill. It may be a weakness and a fear that it's time to get over and move beyond. But killing the urge means having to live with the ambiguous, contingent, historical, and interpretive nature of being human. Killing the urge means living within the human— living without supernatural, scientific, or ahistorical transcendence—living without God rooting for our team.

If we take the traditional meaning of the metaphysical urge and the Kafkaesque version together, we see that they both are trying to come to terms with what *DE* calls "fear of the unknown." Sometimes we confront the fear by building a utopian response and sometimes we create a dystopian picture. Confronting the fear by constructing a Theory, a metaphysical panacea, either positive or negative, is to misunderstand the historical, interpretive, and contingent truth of the human condition. The metaphysical urge is the most un-dialectical of urges. It dreams of an end to the dialectic and in this way its aim is to be the ultimate Theory. The metaphysical urge is the myth of a universal that never changes, a universal without mediation that we must discover and adhere to. Rather than being an intrinsic urge to seize ourselves as living beings, it is an urge to discover an ahistorical, intrinsic essence inside the self that corresponds to an ahistorical universal "out there" and with nothing outside of it or beyond it. So whether it is a God who sees all or a Rationality gone totalitarian, it is the urge behind these and the world this urge constructs that must be demystified. And that is exactly what *DE* does.

It does so through philosophical fragments. Stylistically, philosophical fragments unsettle the metaphysical urge to prevent it from congealing. Through the form, as well as genealogical content of the text, we can see that the philosophical point is that *DE* is not a simple critique of instrumental reason, or enlightenment, or myth. It is a critique of conceptual analysis insofar as conceptual analysis rejects or ignores history and dialectics. In other words, the text of *DE* itself pushes back against reification[1] by presenting a variety of negative articulations of transcendence, and in so doing form and content are reconciled. As reconciled, truth can emerge and point us toward a positive construction of enlightenment.

Six of God

Living within a humanistic type of transcendence, a dialectically informed and mediated transcendence, is not to say that we can completely erase the metaphysical urge. For humans do not start off as mature, and both myth and enlightenment almost effortlessly and invisibly transcend toward an absolute. And while we might readily see that myth longs for the intrinsic and the metaphysical, it also just as easily serves instrumental reason. For instrumentality is part of myth. Myth is not just naively intrinsic and mimetic but it is also underdeveloped and unconsciously instrumental. Myth is a tool for self-preservation. The mythic era engaged in mimetic acts to protect the group and secure their food and to live another day. Myths were used, at least in part, for purposes of self-preservation. At some level, instrumental reason was always at work here.

And although enlightenment, understood as the "advance of thought," naturally fits with instrumental reason, it also can become mythic and metaphysical. Enlightenment dismisses myth because it "has always regarded anthropomorphism, the projection of subjective properties onto nature, as the basis of myth." (4). It regards supernatural spirits and demons as nothing but "reflections of human beings who allow themselves to be frightened by natural phenomena." (4) It reduces all mythical figures "to a single common denominator, the subject." (4) So instead of searching for God, enlightenment searches for truth. This search for truth assumes an enlightenment metaphysics and is a version of cosmology in that "only what can be encompassed by unity has the status of an existent or an event; its ideal is the system from which everything and anything follows." (4) So underneath this "advance of thought" is the same logic that is within myth and this is why *DE* can say myth and enlightenment are hopelessly intertwined. Not only does enlightenment reason develop out of myth, but it develops consistently with myth. As structurally consistent with myth one

1 I'm following Lukács's meaning of reification here.

can say, so to speak, that myth develops out of enlightenment reason. In this way myth was already enlightenment.

Historically, rational explanations and indeed philosophy itself, comes after mythic ways of thinking and forges their being from myth. Still we must be careful not to commit the genetic fallacy. To say that enlightenment grows out of myth is not to say that enlightenment cannot transcend its origin. Enlightenment could, and at moments has, dialectically escaped mythic fear. It has moments of rationality. But for a philosophy that insists on acknowledging history, and, in fact, insisting we are always already within history, Horkheimer and Adorno cannot deny the historical fact that modernity has unwittingly exacerbated the entanglement of myth and enlightenment. But to say that *DE* stays within history and so cannot allow itself a Platonic escapism is not to say that it lacks grounding for its critique or that it commits a "performative contradiction" (as some like Habermas claim[1]). For not all grounding need be universal or theoretical in nature. We can critique moments of history without claiming an ahistorical standpoint. And one can criticize something while also recognizing one's own limitations and shortcomings. For example, writing as a means of communication cannot be considered a universally perfect way to communicate. Still, clearly, we can still write and communicate. Further we can say that writing is bound to lead to misinterpretation, without having to say that therefore writing is hopelessly problematic. From *DE*'s standpoint the concern is not so much lack of clarity. Lack of clarity is fine, for it keeps us modest and helps prevent us from thinking we understand more than we do. It also guards against premature reconciliation. *DE* is more concerned with too much clarity. Too much clarity is a sign of mythic fear. Quick, clear, and confident answers are a sure sign that something important is being left out or forgotten. "False clarity is only another name for myth." (xvii) A dialectically astute standpoint calls for interpretive modesty, consciousness, and self-reflection. *DE*, understood as philosophical fragments, understood as employing determinate negation, makes the grounding (if you want to call it that) a dialectical grounding. This means that rather than claiming some privileged Archimedean point, "grounding" comes from contrast, from a determinate difference, which allows for the recognition of alternative human possibilities. Dialectics insists that something is what it is not, and this "what it is not" provides all the so-called grounding necessary for critique. Dialectical grounding, which is really anti-grounding, allows for more radical possibilities, it allows for truth to emerge in a way that a Platonic grounding cannot. True representations of the dialectic are rational. This is the truth in

---

1 Habermas, *The Philosophical Discourse of Modernity* (Cambridge: The MIT Press, 1992) Ch. V.

Hegel's assertion that "the real is the rational and the rational is the real." A historically informed and rational representation of truth can help uncover new historical possibilities for human enlightenment.[1] True representations then expose what we can rationally create in our age without positing unchanging metaphysical fictions like "God," "Enlightenment," or "Reason." More needs to be said concerning dialectics, but this must come later, as it does within the text of DE itself. In any case, at this point, the important insight in DE's dialectical analysis is that there has been a structural and historical continuity between myth and enlightenment in actual existing human history.

For as we will further see as we go deeper into DE, history has played out in such a manner that enlightenment denies the structural continuity. But running from something is often the surest way to not escape it. So it is not surprising when enlightenment reverts to myth by elevating instrumental reason to godlike status. For underneath both myth and enlightenment the goal is self-preservation and this value quickly seems to trump, and in fact make taboo, any deeper meaning or higher values to the world. For both myth and enlightenment: "Nothing is allowed to remain outside, since the mere idea of the 'outside' is the real source of fear." (11)

We need to look more closely at this. As was said above, myth may seem like an attempt to intrinsically capture and conform to the world, yet when you look deeper, the attempt to intrinsically capture and conform to the world is also a ploy to survive. We did not start out as these pure philosophical creatures seeking contemplative knowledge, seeking knowledge for its own sake. Rather we were largely nothing but mammals, trying to cope and survive in the buzzing, blooming world we found ourselves in. And for a spell the only way to cope, survive, and slow the world was to mimic, worship, and bow to it.

But then we discovered another route to survive. Disenchant the world and treat it as something to be manipulated for human ends. Disenchantment turns out to be very effective for surviving nature. Yet when you look more closely at enlightenment thinking, we see that even as it disenchants the world and consciously asserts its instrumental role, it holds on to an aspect of mythic ideology. And it can turn into myth as one comes to believe that instrumental reason is a panacea. If everything and everyone must now prove their instrumental worth, then strategic reason has taken on a myth-like status. Enlightenment becomes a myth that cannot be challenged or questioned. Disenchantment becomes the only way to discover truth. And suddenly there is this thing called scientific truth that will set you free and

---

1 Forster's essay "Dialectic of Enlightenment as Genealogy Critique" in Telos 2001 (12) makes a similar point, although I'm not comfortable calling the DE "genealogy critique."

secure the absolute. Positivism or scientism, as it's called now, becomes a religious quest that doesn't trust anything outside itself. Sometimes this takes the form of true believers, those like Sam Harris, Malcolm Gladwell, and Richard Dawkins, with their clever, idiosyncratic versions of scientism. And sometimes, like many of the clergy, those who worship instrumental reason, at the church of science, do so because it's our intellectual fashion. In either case the result is the same; science is the new God that penetrates all areas of existence. Instrumental reason, because it is so effective at aiding us in self-preservation, is used to try to answer all life's questions; it becomes the source for meaning, values, morality, and even aesthetics. In this way DE can correctly say "enlightenment is totalitarian" (18) it is "mythical fear radicalized." (11)

"For enlightenment is totalitarian as only a system can be. Its untruth does not lie in the analytical method...but in its assumption that the trial is pre-judged." (18) Just as myth pre-judges that the gods are acting behind our backs, enlightenment pre-judges that the ability to predict and control nature is the sign of truth. Both myth and enlightenment become abstractions that humans must bow to. Just as myth culminates in an abstract, monotheistic God, enlightenment culminates in abstract, data-driven numbers. Mathematics becomes the answer to the riddle of self-preservation and human meaning. Mathematics reduces the world to one controllable thing. It becomes the answer to the metaphysical urge since it quells fear of the unknown by reducing everything to its quantification. "Nature...is what can be registered mathematically"...and in the "preemptive identification of the thoroughly mathematized world with truth, enlightenment believes itself safe from the return of the mythical. It equates thought with mathematics. The latter is thereby cut loose, as it were, turned into an absolute authority." (18) As the authority it ends up detecting myth "in any human utterance which has no place in the functional context of self-preservation." (22)

But when self-preservation is all that really matters, then enlightenment, which was supposed to allow the individual to be the master, ends up a slave to the natural drive to preserve one's life. The individual has lost its claim to have risen above nature. It has made it taboo to attribute any other meaning or values to the world, and so it reduces itself to a pawn of blind nature. Expecting science to answer all the important questions, or reducing the important questions to self-preservation, reveals itself to be nothing but a desire to quench the metaphysical urge, to appease the fear.

Further, in the quest for self-preservation, the "enlightened" individual is serving an unattainable master. It's unattainable because father time is undefeated. No one cheats death. No one preserves themselves and so sacrificing lived life in the name of self-preservation is as absurd as worshiping a non-existent God to gain ones immortality. Immortality is a game nobody wins and yet many play.[1] The metaphysical urge is the Royal Flush of this poker game and like poker the metaphysical urge, the quest for immortality, is a waste of a human life. These games are built on a house of cards that trigger an adrenaline rush, that gets the heart pumping, that makes people feel alive, but so does war. And a house of cards, like most wars, end in ruin.

All these tactics, both mythic assimilation and strategic enlightenment, betray a longing to satisfy the metaphysical urge. It's tricky with enlightenment because, unlike myth, enlightenment officially denies any adherence to the metaphysical urge. It claims to be neutral and non-metaphysical. But such "neutrality is more metaphysical than metaphysics." (17) Enlightenment trusts it can predict and control nature because it assumes an unchanging, metaphysical certainty to the world. In other words, it conceives of the world as a place where instrumental reason can solve life's ultimate problems. So while myth locates the metaphysical urge in some supernatural agent, enlightenment grounds the urge in scientific truth. At its root, belief in the transcendent power of science is just a sublimated version of belief in the power of God. In the end then, myth and enlightenment draw from the same playbook, a playbook written to teach someone how to catch, capture, and score the metaphysical urge.

Fear Factor

The metaphysical urge comes out in the most modern of situations. In game two of the 2012 playoffs against the Atlantic Hawks Paul Pierce had a monster game. He scored 36 points and grabbed 14 rebounds as he dominated the court.[2] Late in the game he was fouled and had to shoot pressure free throws in this hotly contested game. After hitting the pair of clutch free throws to ice the game Pierce skipped backwards to the Hawk's logo and dropped into his version of "Tebowing." Pierce's mimetic performance at half court during the basketball game makes it hard to deny that sports "are themselves becoming metaphysics, an ideological curtain, within the social whole, behind which real doom is gathering." (xviii) Pierce said afterwards. "You like to thank God, you know, for putting you in these positions. It's not pre-scripted. It just came to me." [3] Pierce's moment was instinctual, but it was instinctual only because he has clearly watched Tebow, clearly practiced the genuflection, and so could do it in a moment of triumph; it

---

1 For an interesting critique of the quest for immortality see John Gray's *The Immortalization Commission*.
2 http://bleacherreport.com/articles/1169405-paul-pierces-tebowing-diss-in-game-2-proves-some-nba-stars-never-grow-up
3 http://www.cbssports.com/nba/blog/eye-on-basketball/18927132

was a monument to instrumental reason. A cynic might say that if it came naturally then religion has been reduced to an instrumental instigator and lackey for capitalism. In any case Pierce's antics were clearly meant to taunt the opposing fans, stick it to the other team, and promote his brand, and it worked. It caused a buzz and got him more publicity. Sports and religion blend as effortlessly as the Celtics "Big Three" once did. Unfortunately for Pierce his devotion was not strong enough to carry the team through the next round of the playoffs.

Even the great Phil Jackson fell victim to a sports version of the metaphysical urge. He's probably the greatest coach in NBA history but, of course, it really helped that he had players like Michael Jordan, Shaquille O'Neal, and Kobe Bryant. But despite having great talent Phil Jackson still seems to believe it's the "system" that holds the truth to his success. The triangle offense is Jackson's version of an unchanging universal that corresponds with basketball reality. The actual players and their skills are of secondary importance to the system. In reality it's clear that there's nothing magical about the triangle offense. It's a good system but not essentially better than many other ways to play basketball. But what it does do is allow Jackson to believe in himself, it allows him to believe that he has an advantage that he and Tex Winters can exploit. It is his metaphysical myth holding his basketball reality together. Whether this myth can survive its test in New York, only time will tell. In any case, one can see here how the metaphysical urge really is nothing but a fiction that takes some of the burden off the individual trying to be great, trying to create. It decenters the human. There are short term advantages to this but ultimately it's dangerous when humans think there is a greater obligation "out there" to adhere to or conform to. It rationalizes a lot of bad behavior. At this point in human history we should be able to live without such nonsense. For clearly there is no one true basketball system while every other system is false. Just like there is no one true metaphysical reality explaining everything while everything else is false. All systems and all theories have their pros and cons, and work better or worse, depending on the individuals or players involved, as well as the goals pursued. We should always be ready to modify our system or even give it up if it goes against human interests. And we should be ready to give up the metaphysical urge as it clearly goes against human interest and truth.

And we are giving it up. Not all people or athletes insist that their talents have a metaphysical helper or carry with it the burden of divine importance. It is clear that in our everyday lives we can create goals and pursue projects without asking metaphysical questions or narcissistically elevating them to God's concern. We can acknowledge that our desires and interests come from the past, from traditions, from our historical circumstances, without insisting a Big Guy has a plan for us. We can still see some of our current utopian impulses in ancient religious beliefs without this insight invalidating our utopian hopes and without thinking religion is literally true. Many of us can acknowledge that our utopian hopes and desires at least partly stem from an unrealistic, infantile place and yet can be the building blocks to a better and more beautiful future. Only those trying to run from their lives and from life's contingencies would think that progress has not and cannot be made in our human world, regardless of whether anything bigger is going on or not. Only those who want a guarantee that the progress made will not ever be lost despair over our lack of certainty or grounding. And, of course, both individually and collectively, at some point, it ultimately will be lost forever.

As such modernity seems to vacillate between ironic nihilism and dubious metaphysical foundations and yet, in some ways, modernity doesn't really seem to be a problem at all. Most people have held onto many of their religious traditions and ancient, metaphysical beliefs without coming off as kooky. Tim Tebow can be a success in the modern world, and only has to endure minor teasing (and that's more because he's a virgin than religious). Modernity is no problem for him. And those who don't look to the past for grounding can look to the future. One constantly hears "don't worry technology will solve it" or "we are getting closer and closer to achieving immortality" etc. The demystification of religion has not made most peoples' lives seem meaningless. And then there are those last men who don't seriously think about what it all adds up to or are comfortable ironically laughing in the face of nihilism. Perhaps they are content concerning themselves with the "small" tasks they have chosen or accepted, and don't worry about if it all adds up to something bigger and eternal. The golf course perhaps does the meaning giving work that religion and science do for the other groups.

Yet eventually it becomes a problem for everyone as human knowledge increases and capitalism advances across the globe. In 2015 it takes a willfully ignorant leap of faith to keep believing in metaphysical certainties as religion continues to add up to nothing. Religion is more instrumental than not and so the sorts of meaning it will cultivate won't free us. In terms of the science hopefuls John Gray[1] is right that ultimately science is about control and not meaning, so at best it can be a tool and used as a means for helping one live a comfortable life but never the end. The ends often get forgotten. Science and technology just as often seem to distract people from what's meaningful and important as much as it helps them find it. As more and more people are finding out, texting, tweeting, Facebook, iPhones, and the internet are

1 John Gray, *The Immortalization Commission* (New York: Farrar, Straus and Giroux, 2011).

not roads to freedom, happiness, and meaningful interaction. And finally for those who hope to escape the questions of meaning and reconciliation completely by absorbing themselves in golf need to take a look at Tiger Woods. Living the life of the last man might ultimately put you in last place.

The problem of modernity is still a problem. In the show *Fear Factor*, contestants liked to believe fear was not a factor for them. But for more contestants than not, fear was a factor. Most could not finish the tasks despite believing they would and despite their best efforts. And even the winners did not really win much. They felt successful, since as Horkheimer and Adorno have taught us, instrumental reason is a master at fooling us into believing self-preservation and instrumental success are the highest goods. So between winning the contest (preserving oneself so to speak) and receiving a decent amount of money, one can bamboozle oneself about facing fear. But really the show was about fake fear. No one was really in danger; no one was really challenged or tested. You didn't have to study or train for the show (although it would have helped a bit). These shows are just filler between commercials. Only in a society that is not facing its real fears and not confronting human meaning would people walk around in "no fear" tee shirts and drive cars with "fear this" bumper stickers. Only in a society not facing reality would we see "not of this world" stickers on expensive SUVs and witness others wearing "Jesus is my homeboy" T-shirts. We are sold fake meaning and false freedom from fear by American capitalism and Christianity. And although for a while drone attacks might be able to take out the fanatics who reject modernity and our way of life outright, our faith in this as a long-term strategy is rightfully tepid, knowing what will happen if they get the bomb. And while we can keep rooting for Tebow when he plays for our team our faith in him quickly and rightfully disappears when we see the chance to get Peyton Manning. But Manning himself, like human reason, can be pretty boring, has an arm that is getting weaker, and doesn't always win the big game. And when things go south the Siren's metaphysical song starts playing in the background, and if we are not careful we are again quickly seduced by it.

One of the central claims of *DE* is that we live in an age where both technoscience and organized religion play the role of seducer. They are commodities promising an unhearable Siren's song. When push comes to shove, both find capitalism unproblematic and neither see how they have been corrupted by it. By limiting themselves to what's directly at hand, to what they want to be true, to what's socially acceptable, to what's profitable, science and religion encourage us to sacrifice thought to the machine of capitalism and in so doing enlightenment has "forfeited its own realization." (33) Against this *DE* asserts that we need to see that technological science and religion in America form a social context that induces blindness. Seeing again is not just a sociological question of getting technology under control or of cultivating a tolerant version of religion; of keeping separation of Church and State. Rather it is to see that both technoscience and religion create an ideological curtain that congeals into a: "mythical scientific respect of peoples for the given reality, which they themselves constantly create"... until it "finally becomes itself a positive fact, a fortress before which even the revolutionary imagination feels shamed as utopianism, and degenerates to a compliant trust in the objective tendency of history." (33) How many people think God or science will save us? We need to see beyond the givens of science and religion; we need to see and see beyond the barbarism of capitalism.

From Cute to Kook

Seeing beyond the barbarism of capitalism today begins with seeing that both science and religion have a problematic faith in an underlying metaphysics holding everything together. In the latter case it is a God securing reality and in the former it is belief in facts that transcend human interpretation. Yet when we start to reject the notion that life can be grounded in metaphysical certainties we can start to ask critical questions about things like faith. Faith is a term people use to feel proud of their unjustified beliefs. It is the quick answer every believer gives when asked how the believer can be certain about God or about what God wants. It's similar to the cliché answer the standard believer gives when confronted with the problem of evil. Without thinking the believer says "free will explains evil" or "there is evil in the world because God didn't want to create robots." Of course these answers are nonsense and a bit comical when the answer comes out as quickly, mechanically, and unthinkingly as the best programmed robot. Faith as a virtue is usually pumped into children at a young age. In children it comes off as cute. Children are praised and rewarded for showing faith. It's adorable to see pious looking children gazing up to the heavens in the same way it's a joy to watch little ones searching rooftops for Santa's sleigh and actually believing they have seen it now and then. And let's be honest, it's the same logic and structure used to convince kids that Santa Claus exists. In the cases of both Santa and God, there is societal legitimation of the faith (we have all seen the outrage when somebody tells a child or a young believer the truth about Santa or God) and some authority figure instills the belief in an impressionable subject. These frontloaded beliefs, combine with the imagination, and literally influence perception. The believer actually sees what he or she has been programmed to see; he or she interprets the experience to conform to what a believer is expected to see. What one is told is out there is seen as there. Perception is ideologically distorted from the start so that believers think God and Santa are giving them a special sneak peek into "true" existence. And, of course, these subjects want it to be true so it's easy to ignore inconsistencies, doubts and counter narratives. Overall, to young minds, these are plausible stories. But when you have a kid who's over ten years old that still believes in Santa and thinks he or she sees Santa on the rooftop, you are starting to have more of a kook than something cute. And so it goes with religion. A forty-year-old, who still believes in the virgin birth, or "sees" God through faith, is not cute; rather, that's a real kook. [1] Just as a 40-year-old virgin is a kook. Tim Tebow and Lolo Jones, the clock is ticking.

DE asserts that when it comes to faith it "is a private concept: it is abolished as faith if it does not continuously assert either its opposition to knowledge or its agreement with it. In being dependent on the limits set to knowledge, it is itself limited....Because faith is unavoidably tied to knowledge as its friend or its foe, faith perpetuates the split in the struggle to overcome knowledge: its fanaticism is the mark of its untruth, the objective admission that anyone who only believes for that reason no longer believes." (14) So the dialectic continues to work through faith. We see the intertwinement of myth and enlightenment in faith. Faith only comes into play where knowledge is absent or when knowledge contradicts the believers' hopes and desires. In this way, rational thought sets the terms and limits for faith. Where there is knowledge there is no faith. Yet the faithful wants it to seem as if faith is a type of knowledge claim, or at least that faith is a type of pre-knowledge. But faith is just a desire for knowledge. If faith was not just a euphemism for childish superstition believers would not feel the urge or necessity to constantly try to rationalize their faith. If they really believed and really only cared about what God thinks, they would not have to continually assert and reassert their faith. Defending one's faith only becomes an issue when one has doubt, when one wants his or her faith to be a knowledge claim but secretly suspects it is not. True believers would not understand faith. They would simply believe. Little children don't have faith that Santa exists. Faith never enters their minds. They just believe. Faith enters when they begin to doubt the narrative. So faith requires that at a certain level you actually don't really believe. Faith is too often just a euphemism for "I want such and such to be true" or "I want to maintain this unjustified belief." Faith was originally something non-believers used to manipulate naive individuals. Now, though, faith has become internalized so that many manipulate themselves into accepting faith as a virtue and they chastise themselves if and when they begin to question their faith. In this way, subjectivity dissolves into The

---

1 I owe Bonnie Lapwood for this phrase.

700 Club or ISIS. In either case, believers use faith to see what they want to see, they learn to perceive God everywhere, and it makes them feel like the chosen ones. Bad behavior, bigotry, and vicious beliefs follow.

Faith often looks for verification in extraordinary accomplishments, like Tebow winning. And with sports one can take this game rather far because it is in the nature of sports for extraordinary things to happen. Amazing sports feats occur just often enough to keep faith alive for those who seek it. Yet the need for verification extends to attempting to convince others, so it's hard not to feel sorry for the poor Christian bees that swarm around the Starbucks with the need to prove to hapless coffee drinkers that Jesus loves them and that if they are not careful they will burn in hell forever. And if you disagree they are often quick to sting you. This is where the violence that accompanies myth overlaps the so-called rational arguments and pious motive for their faith.

Kant tries to make room for faith in modernity by defining it as "trust in the attainment of an aim the promotion of which is a duty but the possibility of the realization of which it is not possible for us to have insight into."[1] But certainly there is no duty to believe in God today, and if we cannot have any insight into a desire's realization, then it's a blind faith. Blind faith is just hope or just what we wish would be the case. Applied to God, then God is nothing but a hope, or a wish, at best. Certainly, in modernity, there is no duty to have blind faith in God or religion. So why hope for God? It gets back to the fear thing.

Contrast this with Sartre, when he talks about counting on "my comrades-in-arms in the struggle, in so far as they are committed, as I am, to a definite, common cause; and in the unity of a party or a group which I can more or less control..." this is "exactly like my reckoning that the train will run or time or that the tram will not be derailed. But I cannot count upon men whom I do not know...I must confine myself to what I can see."[2] Sartre's formulation allows us to talk about hope, doubt, and uncertainty without mucking it up with faith talk. We can trust in some things based on experience and reason without having or needing to conclude there is a metaphysical hand guiding it. Sartre's reasoning exemplifies a true representation of the dialectic.

Faith is intimately connected to the metaphysical urge. It is a way to quell the fear and push the doubt back. If religious faith really is someone crying out "I want this to be true" then it's easy to understand why so many are willing to accept dubious evidence until "The paradox of faith degenerates finally into fraud... and faith's irrationality into rational organization in the

1 Quoted in Habermas, *Between Naturalism and Religion* (Cambridge: Polity Press, 2008) 221-22.
2 Jean-Paul Sartre, "Existentialism is a Humanism" (New York: Citadel Press, 1985) 10-11.

hands of the utterly enlightened as they steer society toward barbarism." (15) If you think this is an exaggeration, listen to your favorite Republican pontificate against climate change. In any case, the metaphysical urge uses faith to hold out hope for some metaphysical truth supposedly out there. It uses circular logic to keep faith alive, for faith says we must trust God for our lives to make sense and when they don't make sense we have to trust God some more, have more faith, that this lack of sense has a sense. Begging to God and begging the question go hand in hand.

So the irony here is that faith is a modern[1] concept. Faith requires a level of enlightenment, a level of knowing that you don't know or you don't truly believe. Faith is just another twist in the dialectic of enlightenment. It gives one courage and direction for action as well as challenges deaths' gaze. But ultimately faith becomes a tool to dominate and instrumentally succeed as the Tebowing phenomenon shows. It's a way to cop out of reality when it doesn't suit ones desires, and an ideological justification and a tool to feel superior and special when one succeeds. Having faith in God means that if I fail: "God is testing me—I must trust God—it's part of God's plan." While if I have success: "God is great!—Praise the Lord—this is the power of God." There is no outcome that would take God out of the meaning of the event. And so there is no getting to the real human meaning of the event. Perhaps faith then is still an opiate in the way Marx meant it.

Those who resent attacks on their faith need to keep in mind what Habermas reminds us of: "The discourse on faith and knowledge emerged from its spiritual cloister only following the anthropocentric turn spurred by humanism in the early modern period. The burden of proof was inverted once factual knowledge became autonomous and no longer had to justify its existence as secular knowledge: religion was brought before the bar of reason. With this, the philosophy of religion was born."[2] Today it's not good enough for people to just justify themselves with faith. Religion, throughout the ages, with its hit man faith, bullied and attacked humanistic impulses. Yet modernity did not try to kill faith or religion. It tried to give it a space to grow within the lifeworld. But a decentered space has not satisfied a faith that claims metaphysical insight and privilege. Faith talk is everywhere and as such it helps keeps the metaphysical urge alive and prevents clear reflection on what life adds up to. Faith is a tool to feel superior, to see what you want to see, an excuse to not reflect, and hence a conversation stopper. Unless it's someone's faith we don't find palatable. Did we admire Bin Laden's faith?

---

1 I'm using "modern" here in the unique sense that Horkheimer and Adorno use it.
2 Habermas, *Between Naturalism and Religion* (Cambridge: Polity Press, 2008) 208.

Pimpin' Ain't Easy[1]

Alvin Plantinga adores faith, but it's faith in a harlot God, a God who scores tricks for modern science. His recent attempt to have a bigger mansion in heaven[2] unwittingly reiterates the intertwinement of myth and enlightenment and its fateful dialectic. Plantinga proudly exclaims, in a phrase that could almost come out of DE, that "there is a superficial conflict but deep concord between science and theistic religion."[3] He thinks his monotheistic religion provides rational grounding for science. He argues that science can gain its certainty if it rests on the Christian doctrine. In another evangelical–instrumental use of a Cartesian idea, Plantinga holds that the Christian God provides a more rational foundation than naturalism for science. If God exists, he argues, it becomes more reasonable for us to believe that we can trust our perceptual and rational faculties and we can therefore trust our scientific theories.

From DE's perspective what this really shows is how totalitarian enlightenment reason has become. Everyone, including the hyper-religious Plantinga, seems compelled to show their metaphysical beliefs are in line with contemporary science and have instrumental value. What books like Plantinga's actually do is to provide ideological cover behind which the real doom is gathering. They colonize the believer's mind and satisfy the childish wish to have one's cake and eat it too. These types of books are driven by the mythic fear of any outside and so the mantra is: "Religion and science are compatible," or "We can be religious and modern," and even "We can be pious and vacation in Vegas." Like medicinal mana from heaven, Plantinga soothes the addict's mind so that nothing will interfere with the religious drug. It's an ugly, rigged game for gambler's, a roulette wheel in which everyone watches the spinning, traveling ball as it bounces pointlessly, yet gives the gambler hope, for who really knows what number it will land on. But behind the game, the gambler, like the rationalizing Christian, is just secretly serving an unacknowledged master. This master, sometimes called global capitalism, marches on largely unnoticed and always protected by the silly debates and rationalizations of modern religion and rigged games. Profane games and sacred rituals play pretend conflict and provide supreme distraction. The games and the debates are pre-judged and rigged so you know Vegas and God always wins. Although meaningless, they occupy the lifeworld and bankrupt the victims, as their money and their lives evaporate. Meanwhile the real conflict behind the curtain gets silently settled as barbarism solidifies into

---

1 I owe Shane Hillyer for this title.
2 Alvin Plantinga, *Where the Conflict Really Lies: Science, Religion, and Naturalism* (Oxford: Oxford Press, 2011).
3 Ibid., ix.

a second nature, until the pious and the professor are both driving BMW's, drinking Bud, and rooting for Kobe. Civilization is silently defeated as the beat of instrumental reason, disguised in seemingly innocuous vacations and religious debates, echoes throughout the lifeworld, until capitalism's barbaric sounds from Katie Perry to One Direction gets mistaken for music. Meanwhile the possibility for any real music, meaningful living, substantial vacations, true individuality, decent books, robust freedom, human justice, or higher civilization gets further pushed away from our moment of history.

As fashionable technology and opportunistic religion colonize our world and prohibit any human meaning and banish any human transcendence we can hear the warning from *DE* that enlightenment was totalitarian and that any "intellectual resistance it encounters merely increases its strength." (3) Since Socrates coaxed Euthyphro into his type of conversation there has been no escaping the enlightenment trap. So that even the Other of instrumental reason feels the need to engage in argumentation until there is no Other of strategic reason. For: "No matter which myths are invoked against it, by being used as arguments they are made to acknowledge the very principle of corrosive rationality of which enlightenment stands accused." (4)

In the desire to explain, to prove its rationality, the instrumental nature of metaphysics is exposed. God will ensure "perceptual and rational faculties,"[1] make you happier, get you to heaven, make you a better person, give you piece of mind, show you the truth, secure science, protect America, and so on. Enlightenment reason is totalitarian and religion cannot help but sell its soul to this devil called instrumental reason. Even the great Luther was forced to agree with Francis Bacon that "knowledge that tendeth but to satisfaction, is but as a courtesan." (2)

Those who really have faith in God, those who really embrace intrinsic worth, would not be so concerned with enlightenment-style argument or with pleasing the profane. An honest metaphysical stance, an intrinsic stance, would have no interest in defending its rationality, in proving its worth to heathens and sheep. An authentic otherworldly transcendence would have irreverence toward rationality, perhaps in the way Kierkegaard advocated in his leap of faith. He delighted in the thought that his faith was folly to the scientist and the philosopher. He knew better than to engage enlightenment reason on reason's turf. For on enlightenment turf religion is just "senseless prattle" (19) and yet religion keeps coming back to science's park to play on, and like Charlie Brown with Lucy, begs to kick the ball, pleads to be let in the game. And the scientist doesn't mind for on the turf of analytic abstraction there is no "need to be atheistic, since objectified thought cannot even pose the question of the existence of God." (19) For "the actual has

---

1 Ibid., See Ch. 9.

become so much the only concern that even the denial of God falls under the same judgment as metaphysics." (19) Religion gets a pass in this knowledge-free zone of modernity. In the zone there is much sound and fury signifying nothing. Meanwhile the progress and decline, the trap of enlightenment, the metaphysical urge, all still haunt us like Hamlet's ghost. We too are doomed to suffer until the "foul crimes done in days of nature are burnt and purged away."[1] In order to kill the binary and break free of the enlightenment trap in the name of reconciliation and meaning we must go back to the foul crime done in days of nature, we must go back to the origin of religion.

Spooks

Horkheimer and Adorno describe the origin of religion as a mistake, a misinterpretation. What "the primitive experiences as supernatural is not a spiritual substance in contradistinction to the material world but the complex concatenation of nature in contrast to its individual link." (10) The overwhelming fear that comes from lack of understanding the complexity and power of nature makes the primitive mind believe that a supernatural force or agent must be acting behind the natural event or actually is the event. The earliest beliefs in the supernatural were never too coherent because the notion of separation or differentiation was not too coherent; even "heaven and hell were linked." (10) Nature and the world's abundance and complexity cannot be easily processed, let alone by the primitive, young, or inexperienced human mind. We see, especially in children, when complicated, difficult or partial events are witnessed, the urge to readily reach for and accept supernatural explanations rather than intricate or even mundane natural accounts of an event. What drives this preference? In a word: fear. An individual or group experience's a cry of terror, triggered by something unfamiliar, and in an attempt to appease this terror the unfamiliar is misinterpreted as something more than nature. Since the frightened mind cannot process this power, as it transcends their lifeworld, they interpret the excess as coming from something that transcends or is outside the natural world.

The first human experience of the supernatural, call it the invention of religion, was not some beautiful experience of oneness, some sense of awe and connection with someone higher, but rather was a reaction to something unknown, scary, and overwhelming. If the origin of the supernatural was a misinterpretation of nature because of fear then the effect is one of "permanently linking horror to holiness." (10) Holiness originates from fear. It is the child of fear. From the false cliché that there are no atheists in foxholes to the way American's flocked to churches after 9/11 this connection

---

1 Shakespeare. *Hamlet* Act 1 Scene V.

might seem obvious. Mythic, supernatural, and, religious ideas stem from the fear of a primitive creature in the face of an incredibly powerful world it is confronted with.

This fear remains stuck to humans as they face the vicissitudes of nature and history. In Hegelian fashion, *DE* reminds us that, in some manner, the history of civilization "is repeated in every childhood." (26) Fear, and its tendency to misinterpret, is a condition that every child falls victim to and with any luck learns to largely overcome. In the darkness children interpret the shadows in all kinds of mistaken ways, but through the process of growing up and learning to see what is really there, many of these shadows come to be seen for what they are: reflections of real existing things that make up our world. They are not outside the world, not transcendent, and are not beyond us. When we realize this, they stop evoking fear, in the way something thought of as otherworldly or supernatural evokes fear. But not all shadows get demystified. Some shadows grow bigger as adults, perhaps well-meaning, offer spiritual interpretations that validate the child's misinterpretation. Sometimes the adults themselves believe in spooks.

Since all societies have unknowns, socialization ensures that every child experiences the pull of the supernatural to some extent, but like baby teeth and bed wetting, individuals can and should outgrow it. But getting older does not equate with growing up, and it's not always in ones' self-interest to give up religion. If you are an atheist good luck getting elected to the homecoming court at one's high school, yet alone running for President of the United States.

In this way Lacan[1] is insightful when he says that our starting point should be that we all actually believe. The myths are in us, and there will always be unexplainable experiences, so the pull of the transcendent is always close. While some contemporary psychologists take the lesson to be that we should just "keep believing,"[2] *DE*, following Nietzsche, offers a more nuanced response. As Nietzsche puts it, "even we knowing ones of today, the godless and antimetaphysical, still take *our* fire from the conflagration kindled by a belief millennia old, the Christian belief, which was also the belief of Plato, that God is truth, that the truth is divine." (90) Yes, we believe, but at the same time we are godless. Yes, we are metaphysical, but it's conditional and all too human. We don't just simply believe and actually we never have just simply believed. Part of us believes and part of us doesn't. We keep changing within the structures and lives we find ourselves in. Sometimes we consciously change and sometimes it just seems to happen. But the point is we always have some standpoint or perspective to evaluate,

---

1 Slavoj Žižek, *How to Read Lacan* (London: W. W. Norton, 2007) Ch. 6.
2 This phrase comes from the work of Rebekah Richert.

reflect, and choose who we are and what we want to become. And we need to remember that when it comes to human history, Christianity and the metaphysical urge were never the starting point, never the foundation, but like everything else in us, they are part of our contingent history, part of our broken little selves. The metaphysical urge comes upon the human stage after the mimetic and the mythical started to seduce us, and our debt extends to all of it. Still we are not determined or fully limited by our past, or by a vulgar beginning, or a misinterpretation, or a mistake.

Religion, at its best, can teach us to think beyond the world we live in. It can expand the imagination and inspire. But when taken as the truth it becomes corrupted. This is why *DE* has an uneasy relationship with the metaphysical urge. We need to keep alive the urge to grow beyond ourselves, to be more than instrumental players, but we need not "keep believing" that this means nonhuman transcendence. Plato and Christianity transcended into the absurd, but the fire that they lit can keep burning without the metaphysical urge, without denying an outside, without becoming totalitarian. Our fire need not transcend into Fire. There is enough absurdity in the real world today without bringing in spooks, but to transcend without spiritual or Platonic regression requires something more like art, it requires dialectical philosophy.

Less Than Nothing[1]

The entry point for dialectical philosophy is language. When Horkheimer and Adorno claim that the experience of mana is simply the "echo of the real preponderance of nature in the weak psyches of primitive people" (10-11) they are talking about the effect language has on us. "If the tree is addressed no longer as simply a tree but as evidence of something else, a location of mana, language expresses the contradiction that it is at the same time itself and something other than itself, identical and not identical. Through the deity speech is transformed from tautology into language." (11) Language is a type of transcendence. To transcend is to see something as more than or different than one previously had. Using language we construct concepts, and conceptualization requires articulating difference and identity through a type of negation. Nothing can be defined without relating or contrasting it to other objects, words, or ideas. Nothing can be defined in isolation, or simply in-itself, and there is no prescripted formula for knowing how and what the relations will be for us. So conceptualization has an artful moment, a dialectical necessity so to speak. Dialectics, and determinate negation specifically, is the condition of possibility to conceptualize at all.

---

1 This is clearly a nod to Žižek. His Hegelian Marxism is admirable, yet I suspect his Lacanian use of "The Real" is a secret longing for the metaphysical urge.

From Hegel to Saussure and Wittgenstein this point has been articulated in various idioms. At this point in history, then, the Hegelian claim that something is what it is not should not be mysterious or controversial. It can be understood as something needing the other (what it is not) to be itself, for it to be intelligible to us. What this other is, what is intelligible to us, is intelligible through a dialectical act of differentiation. This dialectical moment is both a discovery and a creation, it is dependent on history, or as Horkheimer and Adorno put it, dialectics "attributes a temporal core to truth instead of contrasting truth as something invariable to the movement of history." (xi)

Science and religion become problematic when they ignore or deny the conditions and contingency of conceptualization, the interpretive, historical, and artful moment in language. They are what I call artless conceptualization, because one attempts to objectively capture ahistorical, necessary, and true features of an object, and the other seeks to discover God's conceptualization. They elevate their brand of conceptualization to a metaphysical certainty and try to apply it to all areas of existence. Against this reification, DE asserts that conceptualization, that what is "usually defined as the unity of the features of what it subsumes, was rather, from the first, a product of dialectical thinking, in which each thing is what it is only by becoming what it is not." (11) Through language "concept and thing become separate" but the dialectic "remains powerless as long as it emerges from the cry of terror, which is the doubling, the mere tautology of terror itself." (11) Saying "Oh my God!" in a moment of terror is just expressing the terror.

When someone refers to a deity to conceptualize the unknown, it initially gives him or her lots of interpretive space to counter fear, and of course gives power to those who claim knowledge of the supernatural. But it's a tautological interpretation, with consequences for all and privileges for some. By explaining away fear by use of the holy, one is also permanently linking the holy with horror since it's nothing but the naming or articulation of the terror. "The gods cannot take away fear from human beings, the petrified cries of whom they bear as their names." (11) This terror gets exposed in the common commandment: "Fear God!" The power of language is a power that expresses the contradiction of something being itself and not itself, being something other. But reflection and critical thinking are needed to delink from the cry of terror and release it from the gods, for "God is just petrified terror." (13)

But as modernity has put religion more and more on the defensive, instead of reflection and critical thinking, disenchantment has become cynical in that: "There shall be neither mystery nor any desire to reveal mystery." (2) Rather than explanation by deity, we get explanation by number. Nature and the world get reduced to "what can be registered mathematically" and in so doing "enlightenment believes itself safe from the return of the mythical." (18) It "equates thought with mathematics" and in so doing turns math into "an absolute authority."(18) Statistical authority is the new religion and extends everywhere, from business, to sports, to politics, and even to religion. With numbers as rulers "mathematics made thought into a thing" and eliminated the unknown through this act of mimesis "in which thought makes the world resemble itself." (19)

Language, instead of being a sign of the gods, is a sign of the numbers. As sign, language can claim to know nature, but it is not supposed to resemble it. It opposes itself to art, which can imitate, but is not supposed to know. Philosophy, starting with Plato, ranked science above art and arguably even above philosophy itself. Plato's banishment of the poets was also philosophy's banishment of art's claim to knowledge. For art to gain philosophy's respect it needed to show its usefulness, to show it could add bricks to the edifice of knowledge. This is problematic for art, because art tries to influence by likeness, not by sign. An artistic mimesis, an aesthetic likeness, has always attracted a philosophy motivated by utopian considerations. So although mainstream philosophy is seduced by language as sign, radical philosophy, has on occasion, ranked art higher than religion, science, and even philosophy itself. This, according to *DE*, is because art "reenacts the duplication by which the thing appeared as something spiritual, a manifestation of *mana*. That constitutes its aura."(14)

Too often philosophy has been caught in the trap of enlightenment by falling victim either to myth or enlightenment, to a philosophical version of positivistic science or monotheistic religion. We have seen, to expose this, *DE*, following Hegel, appeals to "determinate negation." Determinate negation shares with authentic art the ability to transcend the given for other potential human meanings. It rejects simple affirmative language that fearfully, and un-dialectically, transcends to the supernatural like religion, or merely seeks to discover essential facts and necessarily true attributes like science. For underneath both science and religion, in actual existing enlightenment, hides the metaphysical urge. This urge is un-dialectical as it denies anything outside itself either in theory or in practice. This is the real critique of the *Dialectic of Enlightenment*. It is not an attack on reason or enlightenment per say, but rather on a one-sided and hence false representation of truth. Both science and religion miss the dialectical nature of truth. Against this *DE* pushes us to see through the mystification of the given by rejecting language as sign.

Still, it would be un-dialectical to dismissively reject science and religion outright. For despite the limitations of both, dialectics "does not simply reject imperfect representations of the absolute" (18) rather the "dialectic discloses each image as script. It teaches us to read from its features the admission of falseness which cancels its power and hands it over to truth. Language thereby becomes more than a mere system of signs." (18) *DE* wants to break the false dualism of myth and enlightenment, of science and religion, through a dialectical demystification of those limiting interpretations. It aims to show that mythic and instrumental interpretations, when taken as the true or essential meaning of the thing, falsify it. By disclosing the script of science and religion, the aim is not to give a factual reading of history, but rather to expose the imperfections and limitations of these readings and cancel their unjustified power.

Canceling the power of the given is not just a straightforward existential act of inventing new interpretations and making different choices. It's not simply in seeing that one is a free agent and then choosing from a newer and bigger list of possibilities. Žižek is on the right track with his anti-existential reading.[1] He suggests that *DE* should be read as an act of projecting us into the future, where enlightenment will become totalitarian, to prompt us into action today. But Žižek, perhaps, underestimates the seriousness with which Horkheimer and Adorno utter "enlightenment is totalitarian." (4) *DE* doesn't project into the future, it projects dialectically into the past, into the hidden history of the metaphysical urge, and as we saw in our first chapter, specifically into the fictional ancient past of *The Odyssey*. *DE*'s artistic–philosophical musings are attempts to break free from the power of our un-dialectical present, our reified moment. In other words *DE* "projects backwards" so we see into the dialectic of enlightenment and its conceptual and historical journey from the ancient world to the present totalitarian incarnation, as capitalism has incorporated science and religion into its structure and reduced them to their instrumental value. *DE* traces this conceptually and historically to challenge the metaphysical urge. Through an artful–dialectical, yet philosophically rigorous, analysis of enlightenment, *DE* aims to break the spell of the given by blowing up the reified concepts of science and religion, and exposing their contingent and ideological features.[2] Under the superstructure of the reified concepts, we find the problematic metaphysical urge hidden in language. Freed from this petrified terror, language becomes more than a system of signs, and the power of determinate negation gets unleashed. For the power of this thinking is thinking unchained from power. Things like meaning, happiness, utopia, love, and reconciliation are not things obtained directly by power, defined individually, or achieved instrumentally, and are not things a capitalist society can grant.

1 Žižek, *The Puppet and the Dwarf* (Cambridge: The MIT Press, 2003) 164.
2 My interpretation was aided by Forster's excellent essay "Dialectic of Enlightenment as Genealogy Critique" in Telos 2001 (12).

The true power of *DE* then is in dissolving power, dissolving the metaphysical urge, to reveal potential "social, historical, and human meaning." (20) A slow reading of *DE* cultivates the dialectical self-reflection necessary to demystify concepts, the world, others, and ourselves by showing, through a negative transcendence, the positive side of enlightenment that "distinguishes enlightenment from the positivist decay." (18) It points to a richer notion of enlightenment than dominant religion and scientific reason has allowed in actual, existing modernity.

Against science's insistence on language as sign, and religion's insistence on faith and nonhuman meaning, true enlightenment philosophy shows it's possible: "To grasp existing things as such, not merely to note their abstract spatial-temporal relationships, by which they can then be seized, but, on the contrary, to think of them as surface, as mediated conceptual moments which are only fulfilled by revealing their social, historical, and human meaning." (20) When this is revealed we can see that: "Knowledge does not consist in mere perception, classification, and calculation but precisely in the determining negation of whatever is directly at hand." (20) So, while this revelation doesn't uncover simple facts or naive otherworldly beliefs, it can explode the trap of enlightenment through a sublime negativity, and lead us out of the aporia of modernity until it means less than nothing.

CHAPTER 3. FROM KANT TO KARDASHIAN

If *The Odyssey* begins *DE*'s genealogical narrative of bourgeois enlightenment, Excursus II extends the critique by analyzing Kant, Sade, and Nietzsche, whose writings "represent the implacable consummation of enlightenment." (xviii) Kant attempts to subjugate everything objective and natural to the sovereign subject, by implanting a scientific and moral rigor to formal reason. Sade and Nietzsche follow Kantian logic until they dissolve the distinction between morality and immorality. We will see that in the end, then, the dialectic has again outwitted us, as the so-called sovereign subject, is itself subjugated and reduced to what is blindly objective and natural.

Kant has long been considered a pivotal figure for the Enlightenment because he articulates the importance of reason and science, of thinking for oneself, of having a healthy distrust for authority, as well as defending human dignity and individual rights. Still, on *DE*'s reading, he falls into the trap of enlightenment in that he, so to speak, completes the Enlightenment Age and destroys it at the same time through his "Copernican Revolution." Kant completes the Enlightenment by securing science and mathematics, but then destroys it by claiming they don't capture true reality. He elevates the self-reflective subject above nature, but then takes the substance out of this rational self. He dangles a metaphysical realm (the noumenal world) temptingly just outside us, and then tells us we can have no knowledge of it. Each of his three critiques invigorates and differentiates reason and yet, at the same time, proves rationality problematic and incapable of unity, and so perpetuates the intertwinement of myth and enlightenment.

In the well-known essay "What is Enlightenment?" Kant says "Enlightenment is man's release from his self-incurred tutelage. Tutelage is man's inability to make use of his understanding without direction from another."[1] This understanding, without direction from the outside, is a type of understanding that is guided by the individual's reason. With reason as guide, the individual, according to Kant, is positioned to transcend nature or any external authority. To maintain the subject's autonomy reason is defined as simply an organ for thinking. Being simply an organ for thinking it cannot posit substantial goals, for to do so is to be seduced by nature, external authority, or myth. Nonetheless Kant argues that formal reason is robust enough to ground morality and secure science.

In the wake of Hume it is understandable that Kant wanted to explain why science and mathematics were so successful at giving us reliable knowledge of the physical world and why it is so difficult to have similar knowledge and agreement about metaphysical, moral, and aesthetic questions. Still, his solution is disheartening for beings trying to be masters, for he tells us our mastery and the reliability of science and mathematics is not because we are so finely tuned to reality, but because we cannot actual penetrate true reality. We are only masters of things as they appear. True, we don't have to just sit back and let reality impose itself on us; the world must conform to our *a priori* forms of intuition and basic categories. The world of objects revolves around our minds. Yet in the end this construction is a mythic one; it rests on the metaphysical urge. Kant just reverses world and mind. He argues that through the rational mind metaphysical certainty can be guaranteed. This mythic assumption, and subsequent construction around it, is where *DE* finds Kant relevant for analysis and critique of Enlightenment rationality and modernity itself.

According to *DE*, Kantian philosophy becomes mythic as self-guided thinking becomes merely "the process of establishing a unified, scientific order and of deriving factual knowledge from principles." (63) Unity lies in self-consistency so that even "perceptions are incorporated into the system." (63) Formal reason adds nothing "but the idea of systematic unity, the formal elements of fixed conceptual relationships." (64) On this model any "substantial objective which might be put forward as a rational insight is, according to the Enlightenment in its strict sense, delusion." (64) The upside to this is that our minds and perceptions get trained to accept scientific reality and we survive largely because of it. "The system which enlightenment aims for is the form of knowledge which most ably deals with the facts, most effectively assists the subject in mastering nature. The system's principles are those of self-preservation." (65) The downside is that with the success of this system, our minds and perceptions more and

---

1 Kant, "What is Enlightenment?" In *Foundations of the Metaphysics of Morals* (New Jersey: Prentice-Hall, 1997) 83.

more lose the ability and motivation to operate outside of the logic of self-preservation.

If reason just deals with facts geared toward human self-preservation, then it cannot give us insight into reality in-itself, nor posit any substantial objectives beyond self-preservation. The result of this, then, is that reason cannot locate morality in the world, nor can formal reason provide substantial goals for action. Still, while ethical decisions cannot be grounded on external authority, one can and must look inward, to one's own autonomous reason. Kant had hoped that through practical reason and self-legislation we would come to see the rationality of the categorical imperative. This would be an act of transcending nature and nature's laws because we would be acting by laws of our own making. These self-made laws would carry us above our desires as physical and biological beings and we would treat humanity, including the self, always as an end and never merely a means.

Yet these self-made laws, according to the logic of the first critique, cannot come from an act of self-reflection. For in the first critique Kant "equates truth with the scientific system," (66) not with self-reflection and "science is a technical operation, as far removed from reflection on its own objectives as is any other form of labor under the pressure of the system."(66) The pressure of the system makes the moral teachings of the Enlightenment incapable of replacing "enfeebled religion by an intellectual motive for enduring within society when material interest no longer suffices." (66-7) Treating others as ends in themselves and never merely as means "has no support within the *Critique*"; any citizen "who renounced a profit out of the Kantian motive of respect for the mere form of the law would not be enlightened but superstitious—a fool." (67)

So the dialectic of enlightenment, working through Kant, explicitly takes self-reflection out of reason. It reduces reason to just an organ to establish unity of an empty self, and to aid in self-preservation, which ends up in the service of "the interest of industrial society." (65) In other words, if cognition must conform to the system's internal logic, and that logic seeks, above all else, self-preservation, it will conform to dominate society until even the "senses are determined by the conceptual apparatus in advance of perception; the citizen sees the world as made *a priori* of the stuff from which he himself constructs it." (65) The trap of enlightenment sets the limits and terms of what even the senses can in any seriousness experience, it ensures that the senses experience the world through an instrumental lens. Attached to this lens is a camera manufactured and stamped on the assembly line called capitalism. What the citizen interprets as self-guided perception is really a compatibilist recording of a world already written, produced, directed, and filmed by the dominant ideology. The citizen feels at home when they are following the script, and so there is little motivation and certainly no reward for going off script. At best then, Kant can be seen as a proto-movie director, for he "intuitively anticipated what Hollywood has consciously put into practice: images are precensored during production by the same standard of understanding which will later determine their reception by viewers." (65) And at worst he is a porn enabler giving birth to the Marquis de Sade.

We ain't nothing but mammals

Like a porn star, perhaps like Sasha Grey[1], attempting to break into mainstream film, Sade seeks legitimacy by mimicking the mainstream enlightenment ideology. Yet, as the sinful side of the enlightenment philosophy coin, he vulgarly extends the Kantian insight of the implications of understanding without direction from another until this insight un-dialectically implodes. More specifically, he censors himself so he never experiences love or reconciliation. We need to step back to show this.

Sade follows Kant in asserting that the individual, in claiming to be above nature, cannot allow any substantial goals, for that would be asserting the power of nature over mind. But then he takes this logic into his solipsistic universe and shows that the individual need not accept the categorical imperative but can and should create his or her (but mainly his)[2] own base morality. Without heaven to guide him, Sade is forced to metaphorically look to hell, to nature, to find truth and guidance for action. His version of Kantian theory then, allows anyone enlightened and not a fool to use reason in the service of every natural interest, and preferably sexual interest. We get a dialectical reversal where rationality, in being simply an organ, conceptually reverts to nature and nature's interests, as reason, as an organ for thinking, gives way to the sexual organ.

Sade, in pushing Kant this far, maintains Kantian logic but unwittingly exposes himself as still trapped in a false dialectic, and shows his own adherence to the metaphysical urge. He turns "the natural" into a metaphysical category. In his conclusion that we cannot elevate above nature, he embraces only nature's brute and vulgar aspects and begins to worship those. For Sade, if we cannot beat nature then we might as well join it. So in Sade, reason has reverted back to myth, as we are forced to worship the facts of nature in order to avoid being duped by anything not of the animal realm. Things like love and religion must be avoided at all costs.

---

1 Sasha Grey apparently was a porn star before joining the television show *Entourage*. I owe Shane Hillyer for this reference.
2 For the time, Sade's writing can be seen as proto-feminist in that it demystifies sex and asserts that there's nothing wrong with women seeking pleasure. Conceptually, though, it mirrors and foreshadows contemporary sexist commodification.

Love and religion are not facts found in nature, so they are taboo on principle. We end up preserving ourselves, but at what cost, and for what purpose? This gets us back to *The Odyssey* and the self sacrificed.

We saw earlier the bourgeois nature of love in Odysseus, and we can now see that Sade rejects love because he takes Odysseus at his word that bourgeois love is love. Both see love as a perverted game. Odysseus stays within acceptable ancient, "bourgeois" morality, while Sade, climbs higher up the same logical ladder. But when he gets to the top of enlightenment logic, rather than making Wittgenstein's move of using the ladder to get to a higher place and then discarding it, Sade jumps to the other side of the ladder and climbs down the perverted side. This ladder is one of extreme instrumentality and materiality, and it cannot understand love outside of its biological role in nature. The idea of a love beyond the carnal, love that self-reflective beings could discover and choose at the same time, is not found in a seemingly objective nature. A love that is not explicitly perceived, not tangible, doesn't exist here. But what does exist is the body, and so Sade, afraid of anything outside his system, simply elevates the body since that is all he finds in nature. By only finding the body in nature, Sade turns sexual pleasure into the highest and only good. Pleasure becomes the principle of choice for a rational individual when the body is all that is left. Love is "taken to be a mask, a rationalization of the physical drive." (85) Any love that is linked to "the deification of the person who bestowed it" (83) is seen as silly superstition. By getting rid of any sort of deification we are left only with bodily pleasure, a sort of deification of the body. Romantic love, tender love, is seen as a dangerous and deluded metaphysics for fools. Sade's invents a "metaphysics of the body," which he thinks protects him from delusion, and which elevates the autonomy of the self, and frees him from all tutelage. But what it really does it trap him in the Enlightenment Age's myth, as his reasoning turns to myth and bounds and gags him to the dark side of the metaphysical urge. The Christian needs its foil; salvation needs sin. Together they deny anything outside their simple and rigid dualism. Both sides see themselves as true, as pure, as essentially different substances. This is the classical mistake of un-dialectical thinking. Knowing that something is itself and not itself is "Introduction to Dialectics 101."

Sade plays his anti-spiritual role completely though and ridicules religion as he does love. Religion insofar as it represses natural sexual impulses, gets attacked ruthlessly by Sade. Religion is an affront to an autonomous pleasure seeking self. By rejecting the authority of morality and religion, by only accepting what he finds in the natural or material world, Sade has no basis or grounding for keeping sexual impulses in check. But then this reveals his deep metaphysical desire and belief in a need for an absolute foundation to guide action. For without these Sade's autonomous subject becomes a slave to nature's drives. Without a foundation, without a God, Sade has nothing to aspire to except sex and pleasure. Sade is reduced to searching for endless combinations in which to use the body as a sexual and pleasure-giving object. But it adds up to nothing; the different combinations become ends in themselves. This culminates today with the pathetic and sinister porn industry endlessly repeating variations of the money shot. Structurally, though, this sexualized, material world that Sade helped launch is consistent with, albeit a perverted version of, our slutty, money-driven society.

But what makes Sade truly significant for the dialectic, then, is that his universe of bodily coordination has been tacitly accepted and assimilated into the mainstream, even into athletics. The modern world has followed Sade so that what begins as the sexual coordination in Sade foreshadows today's athletics with their "precisely coordinated modern sporting squad, in which no member is in doubt over his role and a replacement is held ready for each." (69) This "has its exact counterpart in the sexual teams of Juliette, in which no moment is unused, no body orifice neglected, no function left inactive. In sport, as in all branches of mass culture, a tense, purposive bustle prevails." (69) With Sade, the orgy "prefigures the organization, devoid of any substantial goals, which was to encompass the whole of life." (69) More important in "such events, more than pleasure itself, is the busy pursuit of pleasure, its organization." (69)

More so than the intrinsic meaning of modern events, sports or otherwise, is their exchange value, their instrumental value, and their ability to distract, to label the modern self so that it feels part of something although it has no idea what this something is. Really, what is the meaning of being a member of Raider Nation or being a Dallas Cowboy fan? Sade's philosophy of trying to keep it real ends in attachments to meaningless organizations whose success or failure doesn't truly affect the lives of those following the action. Any sense of reconciliation is imaginary. The fact that the Miami Heat won the championship in 2013 but lost in 2014 doesn't change anything for the average fan. Yet LeBron James seems to be aging wisely as he senses the need for homeland and reconciliation. Going back to Cleveland, in important ways, is going back to his intrinsically good self, that he rediscovered the last couple of years. How far he can go, given the structure he's within, will be interesting to watch. In any case, in this way, sometimes more so than the games themselves, it is identity, growth, and hope, that fans can find inspiring. This transcendence that comes out of the game of basketball cannot be reduced to the game nor delinked from it. It's a human transcendence that balances the intrinsic and the instrumental until this distinction becomes irrelevant. Watching James progress through the stages of mere physically dominant player to sage leader of a Championship team is transcendence enough. But it not just James; all our lives go through stages that offer opportunities for growth and self-reflection. Rather than looking to another world for models of transcendence, we can stay within the human world, for there is always already every imaginable stage of human development in our world. For example one of the interesting things about sports is watching different athletes develop over time. Most professional athletes are rather young, and watching their game and character develop (or not develop) is part of the beauty and fascination with sports in America. But like love and sex, sports can take an irrational turn and twist into a perverted orgy, a meaningless waste of time. Exhibit A is the extra week before the Super Bowl.

But like people who only watch sports so they can bet on the games, Sade really only values sex for the power he can win. These instrumental goals are simply strategies for filling empty time and compensating for lack of meaning. When people are in loving and caring relationships, and engaged in meaningful projects, the ideas of hustle and bustle don't apply. Sade foreshadows our world then because he turned planning into a fetish; as Horkheimer and Adorno put it: Sade exhibits "the bourgeois subject freed from all tutelage." (68) Sade leads to a world of people who are trying to feel special, to entertain themselves, to avoid boredom, to evade being duped, and so immerse themselves in stupid consumption, mindless entertainment, and perverted games and relationships. In the obsessive worry that someone may con them, they con themselves into thinking they are winning because they are not losing. But these sorts of games have no end game, as fantasy spectators never really win, and yet they don't see it because they are too busy watching others lose. This is the secret of class society. As long as there is someone below you, then lack of reconciliation doesn't hurt so badly. And if you are the one below, you are appeased by being allowed vulgarity without guilt. The only thing class society exploits more than the poor Christian fool is the poor atheist fool; this latter fool thinks he's free because he can think dirty thoughts and watch porn on the internet. So the model of wrong society is to distort the desire for reconciliation through obsessive avoidance living, in other words, ridiculous planning alternating with reckless consumption. Instrumental reason full steam ahead is the ideological cover. Shakespeare's "tomorrow, and tomorrow, and tomorrow, creeps in this petty pace from day to day"[1] transposes from existential fear to calming mantra. Society will not be fixed but since everyone is looking to the future, be it in heaven or the spectacle around the corner, the puppet masters are safe, and the existential angst is quelled.

---

1 Shakespeare's *Macbeth* Act 5 Scene 5.

This is the value of Sade for *DE*, for he shows us the naked truth and the social implications of Kant, of Enlightenment: "Reason is the organ of calculation, of planning; it is neutral with regard to ends; its element is coordination. More than a century before the emergence of sport, Sade demonstrated empirically what Kant grounded transcendentally: the affinity between knowledge and planning which has set its stamp of inescapable functionality on a bourgeois existence rationalized even in its breathing spaces." (69) Because of Sade's ability to push Kantian logic to its nihilistic conclusion without fear, Sade foreshadows a world with no substantial goals and "erected an early monument to their planning skills." (68) In this ironic way, then, philosophy is still the mother discipline. Not only does Enlightenment philosophy usher in modernity, but it underpins theoretically the praxis that is capitalist coordination. As modernity becomes more and more addicted to porn, sex, pleasure, and the body, *DE* reminds us that Kant, Sade, and Enlightenment philosophy launched this unenlightened history. The dialectic is now entering its perverted genealogical R-rated stage. What started as Sade's materialist reaction to the metaphysical urge is now exposed as just another myth and a vulgar incarnation of the metaphysical urge. By limiting himself to the here and now, to what he finds in nature, and by refusing to posit or create human goals, Sade can only find pleasure in domination. The fear of the outside has morphed into fear of a reconciled world, fear of a world where everyone treats each other as ends in themselves. A society like this can tolerate porn but not socialism, a society like this won't miss the ice caps but wouldn't miss the Super Bowl, a society like this will let civilization sink into barbarism so long as they can watch *The Bachelor*.

American Beauty

Of course most of the modern world, most of our world, has not succumbed to the vulgar. Despite the success of *Fifty Shades of Grey*, porn and stupid sex are still marginalized. Against religion that thinks people will only be good if they have God, and against nihilists who think there is no Good, *DE* acknowledges that enlightenment has been a civilizing process and today, books like *The Better Angels of Our Nature* validate this. But the point for *DE* is that we have not escaped the aporia of a modernity unwilling to cast off myth and expand enlightenment to get outside. The path goes through enlightenment: "and herein lies our *petitio principii*—that freedom in society is inseparable from enlightenment thinking." (xvi) Still, rather than enlightenment leading to the light, we get the push and pull between myth and enlightenment. If we give up myth we become nihilistic. When nihilism shows its bankruptcy, we revert to myth. "In the modern period enlightenment has released the ideas of harmony and perfection from their hypostatization in a religious Beyond and made them available as criteria for human endeavor within the form of the system," but through Enlightenment rationality it "became purposiveness without purpose, which for that very reason could be harnessed to any end" until today, when it "is planning considered as an end in itself." (69-70)

This instrumental planning needs the binary of myth and enlightenment to keep the metaphysical urge satisfied. It cannot see itself as just a rusty old coin that really cannot buy anything of value. Rather, it must think it's golden. But let's look more deeply at this Cartesian dualism, this mind/body dualism that Sade so clearly defines and exploits. Like the cry of terror that misinterprets excess nature and human potential for the supernatural, that separates physical and spiritual, the separation of sexuality and tenderness in Sade is a false dialectic, a misinterpretation, an oversimplification, and a misunderstanding of human love. "The beauty of a neck or the curve of a hip acts on sexuality not as unhistorical, merely natural facts but as images in which the whole of social experience is contained; this experience harbors an intention toward something different to nature, a love not restricted to sexuality." (85) Love is not just some fiction invented to make sex more accessible, and it is not something that exists outside of sex and the body, as Christian ideology would tell us. Against God and Sade, the truth is that "even the most incorporeal tenderness is transformed sexuality; the hand stroking the hair, the kiss on the brow, which express the rapture of spiritual love, are in pacified form the beating and biting which accompany the sexual act among Australian aborigines." (85)

Sade, in his rush toward carnal pleasure, missed Plato's important lesson in the *Symposium*. In the *Symposium* Plato stresses that romantic and tender love originates from carnal or erotic desire. The sexual desire for a beautiful individual can lead to an ascent into love. In fact, without carnal desire there will be no human love. This does not refute love; rather it positions it within the history of a sexual and sensual being. When we are lucky, when we embrace our civilized selves, our harmonious selves, we see that sexual desire offers the promise of love. It does not have to be an excuse to dominate or instrumentally take. The body is a condition of possibility for higher love. The body is the materiality to form our better selves. We do not have to give in to gross carnal desire or run to Jesus to escape physical desire. We can never outrun sexual desires, completely suppress them, nor eliminate them.[1] And we shouldn't want to. Carnal desire is the condition for true love and reconciled civilization, and to remain love it never leaves physical desire and longing. There is no Cartesian dualism. Sexual desire travels all the way up

---

1 Alexander Nehamas, *Only a Promise of Happiness*. (Princeton: Princeton University Press. 2007). This whole section is influenced by Nehamas's beautiful book.

to love and love goes all the way down to carnal desire, and neither can be reduced to the other. The body cannot be transcended. The enchanting voice links to the moving lips, the radiant scent bounces off the glowing skin, the tender touch emanates from the extended fingertips, the sweet taste dances on the tongue, the beautiful look radiates from the glistening eyes, and the memories, dreams, and loving desires they invoke refutes Cartesian dualism as quickly as Descartes' wax melts by the fire.

As Plato understood, human love is not simple or straightforward. Sometimes it even begins with a perverted desire. The film *American Beauty* opens with a middle-aged man's perverted desire for a beautiful teenaged cheerleader. But this leads to an ascent into civilized love, beauty, and self-reflection. Still, it's a dangerous game. There is no guarantee that the outcome will be civilized. But the reward of human love is worth the risk of engaging with our desires. For the only civilized way to fulfill a loving desire is to engage with it and connect to another person. Inventing God or a metaphysics will not guarantee certainty or satisfy the fear any better than it does in the face of the unknown. And rejecting love and elevating sex and pleasure to an absolute also will not satisfy human beings.

Sade, caught in the web of domination, of denial, sees everyone in the world through a lens of subject/object dualism and cannot transcend into the human dialectic, to the subject/subject. He doesn't understand that human sexual desire is not an urge to dominate another. Rather it is a desire to have another, while at the same time it is a desire to have this other have you too. It is not about instrumentally dominating the other, rather it is a mutual longing for each other. To dominate others is to not love them, and to be dominated is to be not loved. In human love, you want to be as one with the object of your love, not dominate him or her. You cannot separate the desire to have someone from the desire for that someone also to have you. In the end, then, Kant was right. Love is an intertwinement with someone whom you recognize as an end in his or herself just as they recognize this in you.[1] This mutual recognition holds together the contradiction of autonomy and community, until it shows it never was really a contradiction. Rather, the contradiction was to accept the false representation of truth, to accept subject/object dualism. Through the dialectic then, subject/object dualism explodes, and in a creative act of destruction produces the recognition of subject/subject truth. Kant and Sade, then, in dialectical fashion, lead not only to actual existing enlightenment but also, they point, through determinate negation, to a human transcendence of the given. This negative articulation of transcendence reveals a will to mutual power, a will to true

---

1 Ibid., 57.

enlightenment power. True enlightenment power is against power, it is against domination. It is love.

Still, the Enlightenment has resisted that which its metaphysical urge cannot capture. It has resisted the urge to relinquish power outside its sphere. It has resisted the notion that it is not the Truth. "For the Enlightenment, only what can be encompassed by unity has the status of an existent or an event; its ideal is the system from which everything and anything follows. Its rationalist and empiricist versions do not differ on that point. Although the various schools may have interpreted its axioms differently, the structure of unitary science has always been the same." (4) And this structure, a structure of enlightenment seeking power everywhere, seeking to dominate, has spread like a computer virus throughout the culture, and has itself become culture, as culture has increasingly become enlightenment metaphysics.

American Idol

In *DE*'s next chapter, "The Culture Industry: Enlightenment as Mass Deception," we see directly how enlightenment colonizes art and fuses it with entertainment in an instrumental assimilation by the market. This empties the critical and utopian content from the aesthetic as culture regresses to pure ideology. The result is "the idolization of the existing order and of the power by which the technology is controlled." (xix) This idolization, like the show *American Idol*, has only grown more barbaric with each passing year.

At the time of the writing of *DE*, the general sociological view was that, with the demise of religion and tradition and the advance of capitalism and technology, culture was becoming increasing chaotic. Today we hear a similar argument in the form of a claim that we have entered a postmodern phase where culture is chaotic due to the shift from manufacturing to information, ideas, and the virtual. So, rather than assembly line, standardized, and massified culture we have a multiplicity of styles, choices, etc., that results in a new form of chaos as everything is changing too quickly and there are too many choices to structurally center our cultural world. But we will see that *DE*'s argument concerning culture is just as relevant today as when it was written. Neither the so-called demise of religion nor the rise of postmodernism has altered the fundamental structure of the culture industry.

If behind the dialectic of enlightenment lies the metaphysical urge trying to process fear by denying anything outside itself, then it is not surprising that: "Culture today is infecting everything with sameness." (94) It is like Groundhog Day where every year we get the same ritual, only embroidered with the latest fads and gimmicks. But it's the same old game. Just waiting to see if the groundhog sees its shadow or not. Perhaps it does and perhaps it doesn't. In either case, it's just a little longer or a little shorter winter, but the same old of summer will ultimately come, and the same old predictable action films and romantic comedies will arrive, whether we want them to or not. But it's not like in the film *Groundhog Day*. There is no learning curve in which meaning, beauty, and love, get worked out. Rather it is an eternal repetition of the same worn-out formula, a predigested sameness. The only progress is in the ability to continue and in fact increase sales. The sameness takes on an aesthetic significance, for the form in which mass culture presents and ideologically justifies "the false identity of universal and particular" (95) protects current reality and serves up a false reconciliation.

What drives the form of the culture industry is "massification." This massification has two essential aspects. First, the culture industry produces for the masses but not by the masses. Since the motive is profit, the cultural artifact tries to appeal to the widest possible audience. "All mass culture under monopoly is identical." (95) "Films and radio no longer need to present themselves as art. The truth that they are nothing but business is used as an ideology to legitimize the trash they intentionally produce" (95) without apology or guilt. The second aspect of the massification has to do with the development of technology. As Walter Benjamin famously put it, we live in the age of mechanical reproduction. With the ability to mass produce and reproduce culture, the human experience of art and culture is deeply altered. There are positive and negative implications of easy reproduction. The magnificent works that have been produced and continue to be created as technology so rapidly evolves, and the ability of so many to experience so much, cannot be overstated. No longer must one embark on a pilgrimage to experience a work of beauty outside one's community. But with the advance of technology, the sense of awe and the aura is diminished. Profit seeking takes center stage and we end up with a lot of really bad cultural products. How many times have you turned on the television and realized there's nothing worth watching? How many times has the radio, internet, and movie theatre disappointed? Modern society hooks us on mass culture and too often doesn't deliver. "Technical rationality today is the rationality of domination. It is the compulsive character of a society alienated from itself. For the present the technology of the culture industry confines itself to standardization and mass production and sacrifices what once distinguished the logic of the work from that of society." (95) "These adverse effects, however, should not be attributed to the internal laws of technology itself but to its function within the economy today." (95) Technology gives us access to many new devices, but it is not making individuals more free. In fact it seems to be getting more and more difficult to avoid senseless culture and harder and harder to discover new and exciting works of art. Even cell phones, that theoretically could and should be a wonderful and freeing technological advance, are looking more and more like a force of domination and a sign of alienation. It seems everyone needs an iPhone and can't even put it down while driving or turn it off during the night. Watching people tightly holding their little gadgets and stare longingly into them solidifies Foucault's claim that Panopticon-style discipline creates an individual who is merely "the object of information, never a subject in communication."[1]

Alienation conditions individuals to identify with the culture industry's version of the universal. This creates a type of "pseudoindividuality" where: "The peculiarity of the self is a socially conditioned monopoly commodity misrepresented as natural." (125) Little accessories and virtually meaningless new models take center stage as the focus goes to the new iPhone, the latest laptop, the hippest facial hair, the colorful jacket, the neck tattoo, and so on. When individuals cannot create themselves in opposition to mass culture, the conditions for freedom become problematic. As more and more aspects of life come to mimic work, and the human world becomes more and more constructed as a standardized and vacuous commodity, then the individual evaporates, as Sade's sexual metaphysics culminates in a coordinated sex tape starring the ultimate barbaric commodity: Kim Kardashian.

Kant-dashian Logic

The Kardashian's collapse of leisure and life with work is becoming the American way of being-in-the-world. "Even during their leisure time, consumers must orient themselves according to the unity of production." (98) Individuals lose even a modest moment of free, active construction as industry has taken over major spheres of human existence. Neither the individual nor those running the industries are in control as the "planning is in fact imposed on the industry by the inertia of a society irrational despite all its rationalization." (98) Society is driven by a metaphysical–commodity urge that allows nothing outside as "the classification has already been preempted by the schematism of production." (98) In this universal the "details become interchangeable" (98) as modernity has already achieved commodified unity.

In serious art, the particular pushed against the universal. But now a formula supplants the work. It crushes the whole and the parts, because it simply creates order, not connections. Without connections, that link and differentiate the whole and the particular, reconciliation and concrete meaning cannot emerge. Without tension, a false harmony is guaranteed in advance. This false harmony is the logic of Kant's formalism which

---

1 Michel Foucault, *Discipline and Punish*. Alan Sheridan, tr. (New York: Vintage Books, 1977.) 211.

presupposes and guarantees its happy match. With culture, though, it's the market formula. The individual's sense of order is imposed by the outside, by an alien force trying to convince the individual or audience that there is harmony. The order imposed is not grassroots, it doesn't come from lived life, from reflective tradition, or from concrete experience, but comes from other commodities and manufactured artifacts within the culture industry, manufactured artifacts which are not intrinsically meaningful but are merely driven by market considerations. That Rush Limbaugh's ditto-heads cannot even articulate difference and are completely oblivious to the contrived order and the ideological manipulation is proof enough of the death of the subject; at least the death of many under the tutelage of the old technology. With the internet, YouTube, podcasts, etc., the younger generation is perhaps better able to make connections and resist the established order. How long some can maintain this is yet to be seen. The market order and state machine are already pushing rather hard against democratically-inspired internet connections but, as of yet, have not had success in completely killing it, as they desire.

As these new market forces grow and seep into ever more areas of modern life, the order of the market continues to gain power until no space is untouched. When it has gotten to the point that there's now even a television screen on the gas pump, it has become virtually impossible to turn off the sounds of this cultural barbarism. Being everywhere, they blend seamlessly with the world until they produce and reproduce "the world of everyday perception" (99) which stifles the imagination and blocks reflection. Rather than encouraging reflection, consumers are trained to attempt to catch all the grotesque facts and juicy details presented in the news of the day. Whether it is another Republican Benghazi red herring, an outrageous Donald Sterling utterance, a Miley Cyrus selfie, or an inappropriate tweet by an athlete, it's all unsubstantial distraction. The constant banter of the talking heads keeps everyone focused on the nothingness and keeps the masses "alert to ensure that the simple reproduction of mind does not lead on to the expansion of mind." (100) Today with nonstop tweeting and texting, this senseless mimesis makes it debatable as to if there is even reproduction of mind.

With no outside, "nothing can occur that does not bear in advance the trace of the jargon, which is not seen at first glance to be approved." (101) Immediacy tramples on mediation as "the true masters, as both producers and reproducers, are those who speak the jargon with the same free-and-easy relish as if it were the language it has long since silenced." (101) While Fox News continues its dominance as America's most trusted news source, and ESPN's Stephen A. Smith and Skip Bayless spew loud, obnoxious, speculative nonsense, while Oprah continues as America's philosopher, Dr. Oz as our health expert, and Dr. Phil as our mental sage, the jargon of the social jarheads beats in the echo chamber of American culture. Sadly, unlike today's analytic philosopher[1], this aspect of the culture industry has a type of coherence to it, a type of "nonculture to which one might even concede a certain 'unity of style' if it made any sense to speak of a stylized barbarism." (101)

The philosophical point here is that with the collapse of the differentiation and tension between the particular and the universal, we get a manufactured and sterile style resulting in a fake and abstract universal playing pretend reconciliation. "As a result, the style of the culture industry, which has no resistant material to overcome, is at the same time the negation of style. The reconciliation of general and particular, of rules and the specific demands of the subject, through which alone style takes on substance, is nullified by the absence of tension between the poles." (102) This represents the cultural enlightenments way to satisfy the metaphysical urge. If God doesn't do it for you, well, then the cultural gods will. In this way the cultural dialectic is still determined by the cry of terror. Like the supernatural, culture today gives the quick and childlike answer to kill tension and uneasiness in the believer and the consumer. It promises a happy ending, in the form of an all-knowing and all-powerful cultural God, so long as the consuming believers lay down their cash. Still, against this reification, whether supernatural or super-cultural, progressive possibilities germinate.

"Nevertheless, this caricature of style reveals something about the genuine style of the past." (103) In genuine style, style must come organically through the work and through history, whereas in the culture industry style is bought. And the culture industry has the power to buy style, but not the true enlightenment power to actualize style. If style could be reduced to aesthetic regularity like the Romantics thought, then style could be bought. But "unity of style expresses the different structures of social coercion of different periods. The great artists were never those whose works embodied style in its least fractured, most perfect form, but those who adopted style as a rigor to set against the chaotic expression of suffering, as a negative truth." (103) Style is not something that can be bought and then actualized, because it is not instrumentally gotten. We have all seen the catastrophe when someone tries to mimic another person's look and style. Although he or she might be able to purchase the same clothes, shoes, and haircut, that is never enough to create the style. Great artists don't try to purchase style, rather they are driven by the "logic of the subject matter" and will embrace

---

1 As evidenced by the lack of solidarity with the rest of the humanities and the lack of respect from the natural sciences.

"objective tendencies which resist the style they incarnate" if it suits their subject matter. (103) "In every work of art, style is a promise." (103)

The culture industry can pretend to mimic a work of art because art itself has an ideological moment. The promise that style suggests is a promise of truth. But to capture or express truth, an artist must engage the world he or she is part of. So an artwork must at least partly grant the existing world its due and legitimate it. This is the ideological moment. At the same time, it must try to go beyond our world if it is to get to truth. In this struggle of the empirical and the transcendent, style is vital because it is style that precipitates the struggle. So that the "moment in the work of art by which it transcends reality cannot, indeed, be severed from style; that moment, however, does not consist in achieved harmony, in the questionable unity of form and content...but in those traits in which the discrepancy emerges, in the necessary failure of the passionate striving for identity." (103)

The culture industry generally doesn't expose itself to this failure; rather it relies on similarity and mimesis and hence has no authentic substance. "The culture industry has finally posited this imitation as absolute. Being nothing other than style, it divulges style's secret: obedience to the social hierarchy." (103-4) The culture industry has no authentic content itself, which means it has no style that is authentically its own. So in the end, culture turns into bureaucratic administration. The necessary instrumental aspect of all culture, the fact that culture by definition identifies, catalogs, and, classifies artifacts becomes the whole, the universal, in the culture industry. In the culture industry artists are transmuted into bureaucrats for the given order.

So as mass culture unreflectively reclassifies and identifies who we are, the Kantian construction becomes relevant again. For style offers a promise, and, as Alexander Nehamas puts it, the formation of this promise, the formation of style, must begin from a background of principles and rules within the culture.[1] Style is something that begins to be developed before it can be completely articulated, even in the most reflective of situations, and it is not something that one can just adopt or give up on command. But if the world is such that industry logic is dominating the lifeworld, it becomes more and more difficult to create an individual self, an authentic style. Individuality needs uncontaminated spaces to form and it needs interaction with more than one formula, or perspective. It needs an outside that hasn't been predetermined; it needs to push beyond the current understanding of the self.

This is why science and religion are not the protectors of style or individuality. Science is not completely problematic because there are times when the universal can be challenged. Paradigm shifts, as Thomas Kuhn

---

1 Nehamas, 85.

so brilliantly exposed, in science happen. And the particular does exist in tension with the universal. But ultimately science wants to resolve this tension between particular and universal by situating the particular in a theory. The individual experiment should fit with the theoretical model. And theoretically we could imagine that one day science could end. Science, perhaps, could theoretically achieve complete knowledge of the world materially speaking, yet we would still have to ask how we ought to live our lives. In this way, unlike with art and life, science's reconciliation aims at ending history.

Religion is problematic though, because the supernatural is a fictitious universal, and so can be anything, which means it is nothing. Religion is a pretend universal, an artificial style, like the culture industry, that emerged to alleviate fear, give some people power, and grant comfort against things like death. But it is not worthy of us and it is no longer plausible for reflective beings. Against both science and religion, genuine art—the homeland of style and individuality—can never reach the end of history. As long as there are new people, there will always be new ways of imagining what it means to be human. Science and religion can only be ironic metaphors for creating oneself and can never give one style. Creating a life with style is not a target to hit; it is not an instrumental goal to reach or a mimetic moment to copy. It is an anti-metaphysical urge. Style and authentic individuality scares those who long for the metaphysical urge. To them it's like cheating, because those who have cast off the metaphysical urge follow rules the former cannot understand. But to have a style is to follow different rules, rules not limited to the market, or a master. When everything must follow the market formula or God's plan, we have moved from doing things a certain way to the way things are.[1] The way things are reeks of the metaphysical urge, of totalitarianism. Those who want to live by a formula want a world without individuality. The metaphysical urge, like the Kardashians, marks the end of authentic style.

Entertainment Culture

In our world, culture is constantly in danger. "Culture is a paradoxical commodity." (131) There is something funny about the very idea of buying and selling culture. Culture is not a traditional commodity. Culture presents itself as a bonus, it sells itself as something more than a normal artifact. So if you are dissatisfied with a cultural product, it's hard to ask for your money back. Unlike a traditional commodity that, if bad or broken, gets returned, with culture we accept that we are taking a chance. If the film is bad or the game a disappointment, we don't generally ask for a refund or get bothered

---

1 Ibid., 84-91.

in the same way we do with other commodities. Cultural artifacts have an exchange value that is hard to judge. Since we don't really use culture like other commodities, we don't think of the qualities in culture like we think of the qualities in ordinary objects. It is harder to determine whether it was useful for us, or even if we should think in terms of usefulness. Did we enjoy it, or were we transformed? How to even think about it is unclear as culture, as a commodity, easily merges with advertising, and yet it's a peculiar type of selling. Both the use and exchange values take on a different kind of fetish. In fact, there's been a dialectical reversal so that the exchange value gets the most use. Exchange drives the usefulness of the cultural product such that it's gotten to the point that Bishop Berkeley's "to be is to be perceived" is now a truism. The intrinsic qualities, the place of use-value, are at best an afterthought. As such it's getting more and more difficult to determine what the advertising is, and what the cultural entertainment is, and what the art is, and where is the aesthetic. Sometimes commercials are more entertaining, artistic, aesthetic, and, useful than the cultural product itself.

Still, advertising, at least partly, was meant to more directly provide a social service as the focus was on giving knowledge of the product, but now it is more of a show, a flexing of economic muscle, a power move to keep out unwanted competitors. Advertising is a negative principle, a blocking device that keeps us wedded to the culture industry's universal. As we come to more and more accept that advertising is not about informing us about a product, it gets easier for advertisers to lie and to rationalize lying. Today advertisers are not expected to tell the truth. And the power and logic of advertising has seeped into other spheres as modern life becomes one big advertisement.

Culture, style, and individuality have become a type of advertising. Genuine art uses words as substantial carriers of meaning. But advertising and the culture industry uses words as signs. They are devoid of qualities. Meaning has evaporated. When words lose meaning, it's harder to distinguish truth. When words lose meaning and only designate, are only signs, then truth becomes what one says it is. There is no history or experience to validate or refute what is merely a sign. This culminates today in data collection. Data does not hold meaning. Data is abstract, a formula. The blindness and muteness of data "passes over into language itself, which is limited to registering those data." (134) Without a long, highly mediated process of experience, it is much easier to be manipulated, to be fish-hooked. This is the logic of fads. Fads don't give us the time or the experience to understand the significance or meaning. We use words we don't understand until: "the last bond between sedimented experience and language, which still exerted a reconciling influence in dialect in the nineteenth century, is severed." (135) Without these bonds, we turn to the culture industry to copy and model until we have "the compulsive imitation by consumers of cultural commodities which, at the same time, they recognize as false." (136)

The culture industry has built itself as its own universal, as mass culture. But this massification can and has been challenged. We can contrast mass culture with the more traditional distinction between high and low culture. To greatly simplify we can say that high culture is something for the elite and by the elite. One has to be good enough, educated enough, and cultured enough to enjoy high art. The purpose is to express truth through sensualized reason and passion. Both the artist and the art appreciator, according to the logic of high art, find in it a kind of transcendence. At best, works of art are driven by intrinsic and higher motives, and come from something inside oneself, or seem to be something working its way through the self. As Marx said, "Milton produced *Paradise Lost* for the same reason that a silkworm produces silk. It was an activity of his nature."[1]

So-called low culture can also conceptually be distinguished from mass art. Low art has a realness and concreteness about it. It can give people a sense of who they are and how they and their tribe are unique. It can capture a people's style and character. Low culture is for the masses and created by the masses. From local cuisine, to arts and crafts, to community sports and athletic events, fortunate communities can see themselves in their art and culture. Citizens can also participate as the artists, athletes, spectators, appreciators, and builders of sets and fields. Unlike both high and low culture, the massification of culture, the industrialization and commodification of culture, creates consumers and passive spectators. Today most culture that people have access to is created by the elites, for the masses, and the goal is neither sensualized truth nor community expression; rather, the goal is profit. It is not difficult to see why Horkheimer and Adorno labeled it "the culture industry."

As we saw above, in the culture industry, form is structured around the logic of work. Music, television shows, and movies must fit between commercials and must be profitable. The aura is destroyed not only because of the commercial aspects but, in the age of "mechanical reproduction," the idea of an original artwork takes a hit. High art is not practical and low art can be replaced with kitsch products. Even really good television shows like *Breaking Bad* don't get experienced by the masses in mediated, reflective time. Rather, many people, to catch up to the cultural zeitgeist, ended up consuming five seasons of the show over a long weekend, like a fast food

---

1 Karl Marx, *Economic Manuscripts*: Theories of surplus-value Addendum 1 (11 &12).

binge. Culture gets reduced to something manufactured, packaged, and sold to a passive public.

The content of industrial culture follows the form and must adapt to it. This is most easily done when content stresses superficial differences. The fun but silly banter over Craig Segar's latest colorful jacket during an NBA game is evidence of the lack of content. Content provides a mimetic feature so that songs, films, shows, tweets, and Yahoo News are ideological and "predigested." Culture today already looks and sounds like something we already heard or have seen; the stars and celebrities are all the same and they take priority—or become the content themselves. And of course the special effects fill the screen and become talking points to mask the lack of substantial content. The fact that the film *Gravity* was considered a great film attests to the triumph of vacuous content.

In this way the "culture industry endlessly cheats it consumers out of what it endlessly promises." (111) It promises pleasure but is a sexual tease that just flirts, excites, and then runs away. Against the culture industry's vulgar seduction, "genuine works of art were not sexual exhibitions" but "by presenting denial as negative they reversed, as it were, the debasement of the drive and rescued by mediation what had been denied. That is the secret of aesthetic sublimation: to present fulfillment in its brokenness. The culture industry does not sublimate, it suppresses." (111) Whereas genuine works unite love and sex without reducing one to the other, the culture industry exhibits the object of desire and is "pornographic and prudish" (111) at the same time.

Both high art and low art have the ability to unite humanity as humanity, and to give individuals the tools, the experiences, and the imagination to create themselves as authentic individuals. Together they help capture the multifarious nature of being human and show transcendence springing not from above but from a variety of particulars that are living, intellectual, playful, work-like, serious, and ironic. Through the free construction of the particulars, one can begin to connect to the universal and begin to approach that historical universal even while participating in its construction. "Serious art has denied itself to those for whom the hardship and oppression of life make a mockery of seriousness and who must be glad to use the time not spent at the production line in being simply carried along. Light art has accompanied autonomous art as its shadow. It is the social bad conscience of serious art. The truth which the latter could not apprehend because of it social premises give the former an appearance of objective justification. The split between them is itself the truth: it expresses at least the negativity of the culture which is the sum of both spheres. The antithesis can be reconciled least of all by absorbing light art into serious or vice versa." (107-8) This is part of the tragedy of the culture industry: as it tries to collapse high and low art into profit, it destroys both, as effortlessly as it destroys truth.

The culture industry continues to entrench itself into all spheres of human existence and this "tendency is immanent in the principle of entertainment itself, as a principle of bourgeois enlightenment." (115) The need for entertainment is largely created by industry, and "the original affinity between business and entertainment reveals itself in the meaning of entertainment itself: as society's apologia. To be entertained means to be in agreement. Entertainment makes itself possible only by insulating itself from the totality of the social process, making itself stupid and perversely renouncing from the first the inescapable claim of any work, even the most trivial: in its restrictedness to reflect the whole. Amusement always means putting things out of mind, forgetting suffering." (116) Amusement and entertainment are a mark of powerlessness and escape. While typical consumers might think they are escaping their troubles, they are actually escaping from reflection, and from any thought of resisting current reality. Modern amusement then is freedom from thinking itself, and freedom from being a self.

With powerlessness normalized comes the desire to mimic rather than to reflect. Whether it is the believer trying to be a good little shepherd for God, or the citizen and consumer trying to mimic the jargon and wisdom of the political and cultural masters, the effect is the same. The effect on the individual is such that the construction of the self is not a self-construction. The industry sets our tastes, values, hopes, dreams, and aspirations. Product placement is big business, and advertising and brands have swallowed up authentic life. When Coca Cola, with a straight face, can call their product "happiness in a bottle," we know barbarism has come to our house. The ideology of the culture industry "hides itself in probability." (116) "Fortune will shine on a few and the entertainment industry presents itself as ceaselessly in search of talent."(116) Like the probabilistic wager of making it into heaven, shows like *American Idol* exploit this logic so that all the kids with a decent voice (and many without) think they can make it. And if they don't make it, at least someone else did, and the probabilistic–fatalistic logic never gets questioned. You don't want to jinx yourself by being bitter. And if you protest too loudly, Oprah will deny you a seat at her couch. No, it's better to just dial up as many votes as time allows, and the credit card can hold, and ignore truth.

WOD

This willful ignorance of the truth of the machine is not completely irrational. We are all dependent on modern industrial society. "The culture industry, however, reflects society's positive and negative provision for those it administers." (121) Ideology must take into account the fact that at some level every one of us knows we are helpless within the system. Despite the ideology of groups like the NRA, which try to convince us that owning guns will negate our helplessness, most of us know better. Most of us know the NRA itself is part of the modern sales apparatus and manipulates using consumerist–patriotic logic. Most of us know the American gun fetish is a harmful, fear-driven menace. In any case, the system must account for our knowledge, and so it has to cater to us with "no child left behind" and "freedom isn't free" mantras. This is society's way of admitting its irrationality and injustice. Rather than concealing the suffering, the culture industry, like the gun industry, takes pride in looking at it manfully. "Such is the world—so hard, yet therefore so wonderful, so healthy. The lie does not shrink back even from tragedy." (122) The public is constantly told that more tragedies will occur, more terrorists will strike, more cities will flood, more stock markets will crash, more cancers will spread, more global warming will occur.

Rather than preventing tragedy our "enlightened" political and economic leaders prepare us for the next tragedy, and "mass culture does the same with tragedy. Hence the persistent borrowings from art." (122) Since the culture industry has no style, it merely mimics art and the tragic substance of art. By aestheticizing tragedy, our entertainment culture can deflect "the charge that truth is glossed over, whereas in fact it is appropriated with cynical regret." (122) This cynical regret makes misfortune, suffering, and tragedy seem like fate. Hollywood lives on fate-like tales. There is something for everyone, enough fate to go around for all. But genuine tragedy held onto human meaning when it showed a paradoxical heroic and hopeless resistance to a mythical threat. In the bourgeois distortion, people just learn to accept their place in the system. The goal here is to produce customers who don't resist, for then they are reliable and predictable. With this, tragedy is abolished. Tragedy needs the antithesis between individual and society to give it substance. But when this is replaced, and replaced with the ability to survive one's own ruin, tragedy loses its substance. Everybody in our society rises again. All one must do to cleanse one's soul is to feign self-deprecation, go on the talk show circuit, and smile. Americans love a comeback story. Like Odysseus, as long as you tell a good tale, so long as you have your people control the narrative, you will be forgiven, for you are "forgiven," and anyway, the point is now entertainment.

But our ideological entertainment masks the true human pull of entertainment. Entertainment does not completely negate tragedy. In fact, in Odysseus we can see that the legacy of sports harbors tragedy even as it attempts to be purely entertainment. For the legacy of athletics is not pure entertainment. Rather, sports harbor a deeper, more human truth. This becomes clear on the island of Scheria when Odysseus is treated to a display of athletic games by the Phaeacians[1]. The athletic games provide a chance to see Odysseus in his past aspects as a warrior. Athletic games, for the ancient Greeks, were much closer to their lived reality and played tribute to the tragedy of war as well as providing training for combat.[2] Athletics in the *Iliad* and the *Odyssey* were a conscious practice for warfare and as such held the truth of sports. Ancient athletics were not engaged in for the purpose of sport, as we might think of sport today. They were not purely for entertainment or for physical exercise. Instead, they were specifically practice for battle.

For example in the *Iliad*, Book 23, Achilles's dead friend Patroclus is honored by funeral games, athletic games, held in his honor. These games recreated the kinds of maneuvers that Patroklus's fellow soldiers would have to perform on the battlefield. Skills like chariot racing, spear throwing, discus tossing, running, and jumping are all vital on the battlefield, and are, therefore, a stylized kind of practice for battle. These cultural practices did not provide ideological cover for who the ancient Greeks were; rather they contained the truth of who they were. Entertainment was secondary to the real skills being cultivated, and the real tragedies being honored. Sport had a real and living aspect as explicitly central to its practice.

The situation Odysseus faced with the Phaeacians is interesting because both his living self and strategic self get provoked. Odysseus is invited by a young Phaeacian to take part in their games and when Odysseus refuses, another young man, Euryalus, taunts him. This younger generation is already becoming separated from the truth of war and this young man is beginning to confuse style with mere appearance. He mocks Odysseus because he doesn't look athletic. This would be like someone mocking LeBron James for seeming more built for football than for basketball. As any decent scout knows, looks can often be deceiving, as athletes from Steve Nash to Doug Flutie prove. Odysseus gets furious at being compared to a captain of a merchant ship rather than being seen as the warrior he is. Odysseus, as living entity, detests the idea of himself as being something as vulgar as a merchant. In fact the cunning Odysseus, who throughout the whole epic rarely loses his cool, loses it here. This somewhat playful attack actually makes him reveal who he is. Despite the risk to his own life, Odysseus cannot let this pass. Under all his cunning is the desire to really be himself, to actualize himself as a living entity. In words and deeds he proves himself. He explicitly references

---

1 Book 8 of *The Odyssey*.
2 My understanding of the *Iliad* and *Odyssey* was enhanced by listening to Elizabeth Vandiver's lectures "The *Odyssey* of Homer," The Great Courses—The Teaching Company 1999.

the Trojan War and then seizes a discus and throws it farther than anyone competing so far had. He makes it clear that he could destroy them all at any athletic event (except perhaps running); for he has constructed a mental and physical self consistent with his dreamt identity. His theory and practice have come together into a self capable of defeating mere athletes, and in fact, he has actually defeated other warriors and later will rout the suitors. His style is not an accident, a commodity, or artificial. In giving way to emotion, to not letting his true identity be distorted, we see that Odysseus cannot treat sport merely as entertainment. The festive athletic games, in this case, are not an unqualified success then as entertainment, because sports are not yet unqualified entertainment. When sports lose their truth and lose their connection to our better selves then they become mere entertainment and regress to ideology.

Still, today most athletes, coaches, and fans attempt to preserve the beauty, truth, and excellence of athletics. Whether it is in dominant sports like basketball, when teams like The San Antonio Spurs proved that doing it the right way can still get you a championship in 2014, or even in more trendy activities like CrossFit, where people of all shapes and sizes get in "the best shape of their lives," that we see elements of human transcendence. The example of CrossFit is ambiguous; it plays on a mythic notion of getting back to nature, and the idea of a true or natural self. Its dogma is practical functionality and a Paleo diet. It attempts to connect with human historical truth but is clearly ideological. Through it we see how quickly any cultural product can turn into distorted entertainment. From the CrossFit games to shows like American Gladiators, our pursuits of excellence can quickly become regressive, mythic entertainment. But it's not really us; it is a social structure legitimating an industry that offers us nothing but mindless work and distracting entertainment. Our workout of the day (WOD) should be to push back against this industry. For if we do not, our fat might melt off, but so too will tragedy melt, until the "liquidation of tragedy confirms the abolition of the individual." (124)

CHAPTER 4. BLINDNESS

The sparks of hope for modernity that we see throughout *DE* don't flicker so brightly by the time we get to the final chapter. In fact, it turns out that the dialectic, rather than leading anywhere near a positive conception of enlightenment, culminates in the "not merely theoretical but practical tendency toward self-destruction that has been inherent in rationality from the beginning." (xix) This practical tendency could not be ignored with the rise of Nazism, and *DE* treats the historical fact of anti-Semitism to a dialectical analysis that exposes an irrationalism that "derives from the nature of the dominant reason and of the world corresponding to its image." (xix) To uncover this irrationalism requires sketching a "philosophical prehistory of anti-Semitism" (xix) which surprisingly means specifically critiquing Christianity, as well as human perception in general. Yet ultimately, though, it is not surprising as we have come full circle. What started the dialectic, a primitive fear-driven misinterpretation (and misperception) of nature as something supernatural, culminates in its highest myth (Christianity) congealing with capitalism, to create modernity as we know it. Modernity's enlightenment turns out to be barbaric in practice, as instrumental reason, grounded in myth, misinterprets and misperceives, until the world actualizes its own self-destruction.

In the same spirit that Marx so often begins his critiques, the fact that modern labor is alienating, or the fact of the dominance of the commodity form, *DE*'s final chapter starts from the painful yet historical fact of anti-Semitism. That Horkheimer and Adorno had to flee the Nazis to be able to write this book only strengthens their claim that we are witnessing the "reversion of enlightenment civilization to barbarism in reality." (xix) Yet they make it clear that anti-Semitism is merely a symptom of barbarism; the roots of modern barbarism go much deeper. They, of course, go back to the intertwinement of myth and enlightenment. Anti-Semitism is just an extremely perverted outgrowth of the dialectic of enlightenment, an exaggerated consequence of the logic of instrumental reason given god-like status as a metaphysical panacea. In this way anti-Semitism, like enlightenment science and monotheistic religion, is a false projection in which believers create a world in their own image without recognizing they are doing so. So it shares, with enlightenment science and religion, a metaphysical yearning that destroys anything outside itself. Anti-Semitism is driven by the urge "to make everyone the same." (139) This urge, as a reaction to terror, as we have seen, comes at the price of sacrificing innocents and renouncing the best in the self, even when, at this point in history, even anti-Semites seriously doubt the ideology: "In the image of the Jew which the racial nationalists hold up before the world they express their own essence. Their craving is for exclusive ownership, appropriation, unlimited power, and at any price. The Jew, burdened with his tormentor's guilt, mocked as their lord, they nail to the cross, endlessly repeating a sacrifice in whose power they are unable to believe." (137-8)

"Anti-Semitic behavior is unleashed in situations in which blinded people, deprived of subjectivity, are let loose as subjects. Their actions...are lethal yet meaningless." (140) Not only is the behavior barbaric, but it also diminishes humanities hope, for it signals a common ritual of civilization and demonstrates "the impotence of what might have restrained them—reflection, meaning, ultimately truth."(140) The philosophical tools we have to counter anti-Semitism and to negate the metaphysical urge turn out to be too weak, for those drawn to anti-Semitism "find relaxation unbearable because they do not know fulfillment."(140) To find the peace they long for, they search for meaning to fill their nothingness, but not through reflection and critical thought. Rather, they fill their nothingness with their own image, which they do not recognize as their own image, as they endless project this image everywhere. "Anti-Semitism and totality have always been profoundly connected. Blindness encompasses everything because it comprehends nothing."(140-141) This blindness, like in Saramongo's novel of the same name, is a blindness that doesn't experience darkness. Instead it sees a white light; the blind in modernity mistake the white light for sight. It's a vision of totality, a metaphysical urge, wanting everything and comprehending nothing. The whiteness gives anti-Semites the illusion that they are innocent, that they are the victims. They only see themselves but don't recognize themselves or their blindness. Without the ability to acknowledge or perceive darkness in themselves, they cannot see outside themselves. This white light of blindness emanates from their being, so they do not feel their blindness as a lack in themselves; rather they see the lack in the Other. It is the Other that is blind. The Other, who corrupts their pristine whiteness, must be abolished in this distorted vision of reconciliation. Like the Christian dream of the second coming, the purging of sin, and all that is the devil, anti-Semites dream of a new world purged of all that is not them, and that everywhere and always reflects their unfulfilled urge.

This urge has an origin. Chapter one of the *DE* argued that the invention of religion is a misinterpretation of nature; religion posits supernatural explanations when natural ones are too complicated or inconvenient to accept. With the belief in the supernatural comes the creation of other myths culminating in monotheism, and specifically, for the West, Christianity. But Christianity grew out of Judaism and as such is part of the philosophical prehistory of anti-Semitism. While it is obvious that Nazism is anti-Semitic and barbaric, it is not so obvious that Christianity is. But it is obvious that Christianity needs and justifies the metaphysical urge, and this is the root of its anti-Semitism and the true root of Christianity's appeal.

True Religion

As Horkheimer and Adorno see it, most individuals have long ceased to trouble themselves with eternal salvation. Christianity's appeal lies elsewhere. Modern Christians do not spend most of their time reading the bible, praying, and preparing the soul for the afterlife. Cleansing the soul is thought about perhaps on Sundays, during moments of religious holidays, and when death is approaching. But the bulk of the believer's time, energy, and thoughts are occupied by secular things. Yet Christians use religion to get ahead in the world and to position themselves as legitimate and noble, so in reality: "The average believer today is as crafty as only cardinals were in former times."(144) The average believer uses religion like Odysseus. Religious jargon and pious positioning are modes of cunning for many in the modern world. The religious attitude is pre-reflective; it is part of the automated self. These automated selves are just part of the larger social machine that has Christianity built into the America way of life. Religion is an angle for a religious person to feel unique without being unique. It is an imitation without historical understanding, or current knowledge, or self-reflection. It's a chance to wear True Religion jeans. In the believer's mind though, it's never merely about him or her: it's for God, for Jesus, for Truth, for Morality, for the children, for the cause and so on. It's never about his or her will to power or existential fear, but for something higher, for in that way the pious one can rationalize and justify the obnoxious and invasive behavior he or she exposes the rest of us to. It's a socially acceptable way to release existential angst and to advance oneself in modernity without directly admitting you are advancing yourself. One can be anti-Gay, not because Gay people are harming you, but because the Bible says so. A Christian man can purge his emotions in this masculine culture and still be a man if it's directed toward his faith. He can crush his opponent and taunt him so long as he gives God his props. Just say: "I'm blessed and give all the glory to God" and no one can criticize you. Turn on the television and you see grown men pointing to the heavens after a score or weeping uncontrollable over the thought of the crucifixion. And it would only be pathetic and not barbaric if the line from their pious displays to Bin Laden were not so short, if their desire to make everyone follow Jesus did not conceptually lead straight to the gas chambers. From tattoos to bumper stickers, to Christian clothing lines, we see, hear, read, and witness the screams of people attempting to hold onto, validate, and externalize their metaphysical urges, and we see society absorbing this neurosis as if it were normal behavior.

But if we look a little deeper, or happen to be slightly outside that Kool-Aid stand, we see the constrained search for meaning in these now meaningless ancient beliefs, and we see the attempt to forge a self, while denying what this self really is and what it really means. Spirituality today is a renunciation of subjectivity and serves a modern world without subjects and without meaning. Religion today is Odysseus without the homecoming, all dressed up in Christianity with nowhere to go. Floating in the sea of modernity, those who claim supernatural insight are like Odysseus but without an inner self to lament when the Sirens sing, for their "Not of this World" brand satisfies their spiritual taste; for they have no taste. Between the commodification of religion and its social superiority complex, Christianity occupies most of their lifeworld, but never as true religion. One can consume the dogma at the megachurch, the shopping mall, the sporting event, the private school, on television, radio, the internet, and now even through a flood of bad movies. The pious ones can walk tall and proud around America believing they are moral, grounding their values in the Bible, and feeling smug next to the seemingly nihilistic shells that believe in nothing. They can even ground their hatred for Obama in their God. This distorted self-image sustains itself because the "alliance between enlightenment and power has debarred from consciousness the moment of truth in religion while conserving its reified forms." (144) Combining Christianity and right wing politics will "finally benefit fascism" (144) as this reification becomes the common sense of a people treading water and waiting for the great flood to wash big, bad Obama away. Meanwhile, back in reality, Bush's actual flood, New Orleans, doesn't even register in their consciousness.

So despite rumors to the contrary, religion is not in decline in America. Reified Christianity, disguising barbarism, has been seamlessly "incorporated as cultural heritage, not abolished." (144) The Enlightenment debarred the moment of truth in religion, yet religion survives in reified forms. Religion is partly meshed directly into the system and partly transposed into the "pomp of mass culture and parades." (144) Horkheimer and Adorno would see claims by some contemporary philosophers that religion is now the place of doubt and of questioning as rather naive. All the doubting and questioning can't be taken seriously. One has to be willfully ignorant to believe any claims of the supernatural. At this point in history, to have to argue against monotheistic religion is like arguing against witches, dragons, and chimera. Those who believe need a cure, not a refutation. But in a wrong society, the religious ones are seen as healthy, so they never go to the doctor and the cancer grows and spreads throughout the lifeworld.

Consequently, the masses continue to believe, and with a "fanatical faith on which leader and followers pride themselves" (144) and which they wear as badges of honor. The "grim doctrine which was earlier used to discipline the desperate" (144) lingers, but now without the content. Religion in America today is about everything, and religion is only a small part of it. It's about freedom, taxes, politics, sports, culture, friendship, business, education, love, and so on. Athletics, with the emphasis on winning and miraculous results, fits nicely with the religious mind. For in sports it seems anything can happen; sports fuel that crazy religious mentality that defies articulation. Religion slips in and out of modernity like an annual flu virus. To survive, it changes forms but still produces basically the same sickness. If you doubt the lack of content in religion today, just go to a sporting event hosted by a religious institution. The fervor in which they cheer discloses the anemia of their dogma. Beating the Other, more than cultivating a pious self, is where the energy is directed. It is as if winning will validate their faith, as if Jesus would even know or care about such things. This doesn't matter though, because for the believer it's all in the name of praising Jesus, so to hell with what Jesus would really want. Jesus must love a winning team; it's in the bible somewhere, I'm sure. Still, it's hard not to see hatred for opposing teams going hand in hand with hatred for nonbelievers. This is why DE can say, without exaggeration, that "content lives on only as hatred of those who do not share the faith" and "all that remained of the religion of love was anti-Semitism."(144-5) Perhaps today, all that remains is hatred towards those who don't like football, Chevy trucks, or Fox News, hatred for anything perceived as anti-capitalist or un-American.

The terror, originating from the unknown in nature, eventually can only be satisfied by monotheism for those stuck in a supernatural paradigm. Only with an omnipotent, omniscient, and omnibenevolent nonhuman human can the fear-induced, supernatural seeking mind feel safe. The creator and ruler must entirely subjugate nature to quell this type of fear. A perfect God is the ultimate attempt to overcome fear and deny any sense of an outside. The initial misinterpretation that gives rise to the mythic mistake in primordial beings has grown into a leviathan of a perfect Being pulling all the strings of the universe. God as spirit stands completely above and in control of nature and the world, and so offers liberation from it. This is the ultimate attempt to grasp onto something that could finally defeat the contingencies of history and life. This is the metaphysical urge supersized. But belief in this perfectly good, über-powerful and all-knowing nonhuman dude turns out to come with a unique price as Christianity tries to one up all competitors.

It started with trying to one up Judaism. "Christianity is not only a regression beyond Judaism" (145), it also offers an initially cleaner metaphysical alternative. For Judaism "did not entirely shed the features of the nature demon."(145) Although the God of Abraham is conceived of as universal, God is still connected to the profane, material world and to nature in a way that the Christian God is not. The terror from nature moves into the God of Abraham which "as spirit is the principle opposed to nature; it not only stands for nature's blind cycle as do all the mythical gods, but offers liberation from it." (145) But in an ironic dialectic reversal this God becomes more terrifying than nature itself. For this God "tolerates nothing beside itself" (145) and as agent then is more demanding and ambiguous than anonymous fate. At least with nature one can come to understand, predict, and control it. At least with less powerful deities one can slip something past them when they are not looking, or perhaps appeal to a different deity. At least with fate one need not take it personally. Against these, Judaism sets the totalitarian groundwork with its monotheistic terror and totalizing metaphysics.

While Christianity follows Judaism's God that "tolerates nothing beside itself," it also emphasizes the moment of grace. This initially seems to lessen the dread of the absolute of Judaism by allowing the primitive creature to find itself reflected in the deity. Score one point for Christianity and zero for Judaism. A compassionate creator is the form for which grace is the content. To motivate this moment of grace Christianity juts from Judaism with its divine mediator named Jesus. In Jesus, the supernatural is given a human form, a name, and a history, and he seemingly dies a human death. "His message is: fear not; the law yields before faith; love becomes greater than any majesty, the only commandment." (145)

With this move Christianity rushes in to calm the Judeo terror by making the spirit seem humanlike and giving hope that mere mortals might also be spirit like Christ. The goal is to forget that humans are inevitably part of nature. To forget our nature, it helps if we believe that the supernatural, the spirit, is partly flesh like us. This helps sell the possibility of flesh harboring soul. If the spirit can become flesh, well then, perhaps the flesh can become spirit, so to speak. God's grace and compassion makes it all fit so nicely, seem so logical.

But the virtue of a Christianity that lifts the spell of a Jewish religion still too linked with nature also produces a new ideology, but now in a spiritualized form. As the idea of God is brought closer to the finite beings, finite beings are brought closer to God, and to the idea of surviving the death of the body. "Christ, the incarnated spirit, is the deified sorcerer." (145) Jesus, as flesh, is God. Christianity insists that the mortal Jesus was really God. Christianity takes the bold step of humanizing God, not through a link from higher to lower but by reducing God to mortal man. Christianity itself then is reduced to a magic trick. Precisely at the moment when the religion asks one to be reflective, it pulls a Jesus out of a hat and becomes merely the spiritualization of magic. Mind is asked to grant a perfect spiritual essence to a mortal being. Mind is asked to first accept that a God can die like a mortal and at the same time not die like an immortal. Mind is asked to embrace a contradiction as the answer to terror. "Bad conscience is therefore obliged to present the prophet as symbol, the magical practice as transubstantiation." (145-6) In the end then, this monotheistic–magical religion grounds its uniqueness with an intellectually suspect "special sphere of culture." (146)

Unlike Christian voodoo, Judaism was firmly rooted in the national life and survival of the group. Christianity satisfies an atomistic taste, an individualistic, self-preserving sensibility, along the model of laissez-faire capitalism. With Christianity everybody gets a personal savior. Jesus is the guy who tells everybody he's their best friend. He makes everybody feels special. He's the personal savior, the sales guy who comes to your door who really seems to care about you. It's an egotistical and ideological narrative other myths cannot compete with. It's so ridiculous, but repeats itself with such ease and unjustified self-confidence, that it sticks. Sell the big lie long and hard enough and people will believe it; tell the big lie and make it so big no one will question it.

In one sense it is understandable to tell the big lie. Our fear of nature reaches its climax in knowing we will die and in trying to avoid this unhappy fate. But by taking this known fact of life (mortality) and magically denying it, Christianity undercuts its intrinsic and good moment and turns it into a farce. By coming back to life, by rising again, the sacrifice becomes a fake sacrifice. A pretend dying for our sins, in which Christ pays no real price, a death faked with smoke and mirrors like any good magic trick. Yes, he dies, but comes back shortly after and will come back again. Like David Copperfield without the stage charisma, Jesus has another show in Vegas.

Mythic belief systems prior to Christianity generally linked worship, internal belief, and social labor. "In providing the schema for the latter, sacrifice becomes rational."(146) It's not that the rules necessarily arose from rational reflection, it is more like rationality arose from the rules. As primitive people attempted to free themselves from immediate fear, their rituals and institutions became more and more refined, culminating in Judaism's "sanctified rhythm of family and national life."(146) The human root of it all: fear of nature, the solidarity of the group, and the conscious desire for self-preservation, never got completely lost.

But Christianity "wanted to remain spiritual even where it aspired to power. In ideology it repudiated self-preservation by the ultimate sacrifice, that of the man-god, but thereby relegated devalued life to the sphere of the profane." (146) The narrative disclaimed self-preservation by the ultimate sacrifice, but then took it right back by celebrating the spooky resurrection. This is secretly the pinnacle of enlightenment reason, where nothing trumps self-preservation. Death is to be cheated and conquered though the imitation of Christ. If this is the case, self-sacrificing love loses its innocence. The beauty gets stripped away. Pretend to sacrifice power to gain a greater power. Sacrifice worldly life to gain eternal, otherworldly life. Contemporary Christianity is the soulmate to an instrumental world that only values outcomes. The beauty of the religion of love, the nobility of grace, is revealed to be a sham. "In this way self-sacrificing love is stripped of its naïveté, severed from natural love and turned to account as credit." (146) The Christian doctrine of immediate, unconditional love, in which nature and the supernatural reach reconciliation, turns out not to be reconciliation at all, it turns out to be instrumental manipulation and calculation. "Therein lies its untruth: in the fraudulently affirmative interpretation of self-forgetting." (146)

The fraud goes deeper and the self-forgetting has many layers, as Christianity "depends for its existence on people's belief that they will attain salvation by following its teaching" (146); and yet it cannot guarantee that goal. The religious promise of salvation is nonbinding. This is "ignored by naive believers, for whom Christianity, supranaturalism, becomes a magic ritual, a nature religion. They believe only by forgetting their belief. They convince themselves of the certainty of their knowledge like astrologers or spiritualists." (146-7) How many Christians today say they know they are going to heaven? The forgetfulness that they cannot know is suppressed and repressed to keep the religion viable. It breeds an egotistical and paranoid personality that has to overcompensate for the unacknowledged but willful forgetting. This creates a distorted personality. Christian jerk is too often redundant. The belief system creates an arrogant and insecure personality.

Christians hold close the belief that they will be forgiven and they have been chosen, while in fact they cannot know this. They hold the belief that God is love while they dream of preserving the self. To sell to oneself and the world ones dubious faith it helps to paste "forgiven" on the back of the car or a T-shirt; externalizing eases the doubt. Call it the "good news" and you can start believing the linguistic trick.

Prior to the "good news," non-deluded people knew death was the end of life. With the new doctrine the believers are left wondering what will become of them. They have outwitted themselves and entered a deeper unknown. If the fear of mortality was not enough; their Christianity adds the fear of immortality. For no one but God gets to know who goes to heaven. This deeper terror, of possible eternal suffering, is overcompensated for by the believer, in the act of willful forgetting, rationalization, and even complete denial. Christians love to ignorantly proclaim: "heaven is for real" and "I know I'm going to heaven." The doctrine encourages one to not think about the fact that one can never really know and cannot ever adequately grasp who the good news is for. Christ's sacrifice doesn't promise salvation for those in whose name it is made. Even if they play the game: ask for forgiveness, take God into their hearts, walk the walk, do good works, have faith, etc., there is no guarantee that they have been chosen. They still could face eternal damnation and won't know it until after they die. Capitalism's good news also requires that we "forget," that we accept risk, that we internalize it, that we blame ourselves when we don't make it. The "good news" turns out to be the perfect propaganda for our market-based reality.

Still, this seems to work for many Americans. But what works may also make one barbaric. The Christian, as a species, is either skilled in self-deception, psychologically disturbed, or just oblivious. "To the simple, however, religion itself becomes a substitute for religion." (147) Against this regression is a mutant subspecies, those like Pascal and Kierkegaard, who evolved without forgetting or denying the truth of the doctrine. This cultivated a more tolerant and intellectually honest believer. Unfortunately, this later group is an anomaly, as the pull and seduction offered in forgetting is too strong. Against existential Christianity, the "others, who repressed that knowledge and with bad conscience convinced themselves of Christianity as a secure possession, were obliged to confirm their eternal salvation by the worldly ruin of those who refused to make the murky sacrifice of reason. This is the religious origin of anti-Semitism." (147) Rather than looking inward, there is an outward hostility toward those who don't believe. The gaze of the Other is too much, it exposes the weak inner self clinging to its fiction, and so the bigoted Christian's hatred toward the Other is really a fear of truth. These Christians suspect that Jews know better in not accepting the divinity of Jesus. The gaze of the Jew on their childish worship of Jesus disconcerts them. Christians hate Jews and atheists "as one hates those who know better."(147) This hatred also harbors the truth of faith. Faith is hostility towards reflection. Faith is resentment toward anyone who questions spirit. Faith is hatred toward anyone who "withstands evil without rationalizing it." (147) No original sin, no big picture defense, no free will argument can explain evil, and anyone willing to expose that truth must pay for it. Christianity's real meaning then, is "to confirm that the ritual of faith and history is justified by ritually sacrificing those who deny its justice." (147)

The Dude Abides

Unlike the Dude in the Cohen brothers' film *The Big Lebowski*, anti-Semites cannot abide a world they don't understand. "The stock reply of all anti-Semites is the appeal to idiosyncrasy." (147) Anti-Semites cannot accept anything outside their lifeworld, but rather than reflecting on what they cannot abide they appeal to idiosyncrasy. Rather than looking inward and asking why they are bothered by the Other, anti-Semites dismiss their aversion as a personal choice or taste. The philosophical problem here though is that the cure for "anti-Semitism depends on whether the content of that idiosyncrasy is raised to the level of a concept and becomes aware of its own senselessness." (147) In other words, self-reflection is necessary to answer why one cannot tolerate the Other, why one feels the aversion they do. Why does one care that another is different, why is one bothered that another cannot fit into the given conceptual web? Again, to answer this one must raise the content of the idiosyncratic to the level of a concept, and this requires not treating it as an idiosyncratic quirk. Concepts are intersubjective, social, and attach themselves to the universal. But the "idiosyncrasy attaches itself to the peculiar."(147) What is peculiar, unlike the universal, doesn't reach conceptual status and so cannot be analyzed. "The universal, that which fits into the context of social utility, is regarded as natural. But anything natural which has not been absorbed into utility by passing through the cleansing channels of conceptual order...whatever is not quite assimilated, or infringes the commands in which the progress of centuries has been sedimented, is felt as intrusive and arouses a compulsive aversion." (147-8)

So what provokes the compulsive aversion goes unanalyzed. The anti-Semite cannot abide that which seems meaningless. Why should we have to justify or think about why we feel aversion toward something meaningless? They just don't like it; end of story. But really what one is adverse to may not be meaningless. It may just not be instrumentally useful or socially assimilated. Instrumental reason has so beaten down a rational–mimetic way of experiencing the world that when they get even an indirect taste of it, individuals misinterpret or don't consciously interpret at all. They just chalk it up to personal idiosyncratic aversion. The aversion, unknowingly then, rather than just being a personal dislike of something or someone, may really be an aversion toward any sort of mimesis and especially uncontrolled mimesis. What anti-Semites think of as a dislike towards someone Jewish may be a dislike of the mimetic impulse itself, or perhaps dislike of aspects of themselves they cannot acknowledge, or it might be a fear of a more direct connection to nature or others. In any case it doesn't get analyzed because it doesn't fit into the conceptual order of their world. The Other, the one outside the conceptual order, may be a guilty reminder to anti-Semites of a part of themselves ignored and forgotten, a part not captured by enlightenment reason, not captured by an instrumental relation to nature. Rather than admitting and analyzing this, anti-Semites fall back into idiosyncratic rationalization.

"The motifs which trigger such idiosyncrasy are those which allude to origins, they recreate moments of biological prehistory: danger signs which made the hair stand on end, the heart stop, individual organs escape the subject's control, autonomously obeying fundamental biological stimuli. Protection as petrified terror is a form of camouflage."(148) The idiosyncratic aversion harkens back to a time in which we preserved ourselves by giving in to nature, perhaps even against our will. In moments of terror one can lose control, even of parts of one's body and mind. This loss of control may aid us in survival since what takes over may mimic the world and provide camouflage. This mimesis, against enlightenment dogma, contains the truth that we are never completely in control, not even of ourselves. Further it exposes the truth of our connection to nature. The idiosyncratic excuse "protects" us from acknowledging these memories and "protects" us from acknowledging the fact that we cannot completely control even ourselves, let alone the outside we have been denying. At some level we may suspect something more is going on, but without analysis this gets shrugged off. All that remains is a misunderstood fear. As misunderstood, the fear turns into hatred for another, for the Other represents something not acknowledged, and yet endowed with the power to come rushing through the door any second.

It's a bit of a trap, though, for these primitive motifs can no longer be consciously acknowledged by enlightenment or completely gotten rid of. The ego is forced to subsume the motifs under the familiar or reject them as idiosyncratic aversions. In other words, the price we pay for civilization is to repress our desire for mimesis or instrumentally exploit it. "However, the constellation under which sameness is established, both the direct sameness of mimesis and the indirect sameness of synthesis, the adaptation of the self to the thing in the blind act of living no less than the comparison of reified elements in scientific conceptualization—that constellation remains terror." (148-9) These two moments of petrified terror are captured in the attitude of Dennis Miller before and after 9/11. Before that tragic day Miller suppressed his primal fears through humor and a mix of liberal and libertarian ideology, but after the event he couldn't consciously ignore the contingency and absurdity of our world and became dogmatically conservative and tribal; became mythic fear conservatively radicalized.

Contemporary societies preferred manner of processing fear, of establishing sameness, of satisfying the metaphysical urge, is through numbers. "The mathematical formula is consciously manipulated regression, just as the magic ritual was; it is the most sublimated form of mimicry." (149) Today the fetish for assessment, and data driven outcomes, completes the fetish for conceptual universals that have social utility. With the inability to process non-instrumental difference the result is "the blind mastery of nature, which is identical to farsighted instrumentality." (149) Missing the concrete realness in front of us requires that we not clearly see ourselves or others. "Those blinded by civilization have contact with their own tabooed mimetic traits only through certain gestures and forms of behavior they encounter in others, as isolated, shameful residues in their rationalized environment. What repels them as alien is all too familiar."(149) So it must be denied and destroyed.

But what exactly is being denied and destroyed? It is the freedom of a self that cannot be reduced to a universal category. It is the freedom to push back against the god called self-preservation in the name of subjectivity. It is the freedom that comes from consciously living in the moment, from intrinsically meaningful activity, while at the same time, projecting instrumentally in a reconciled manner. It is the freedom to allow your best self to develop even at the cost of instrumental success. The balance, the intertwinement of the intrinsic and the instrumental, preserves dialectical truth but there are many ways to get it wrong. Historically we err on the side of the instrumental, and given that the intrinsic has been suppressed or exploited regularly it too often only comes out in an infantile form. A rational mimesis does not simply imitate without reflection. Rather it learns through listening to the Other, as another, and not as something to be used. It intrinsically wants to understand, communicate, and reach consensus. This type of mimesis promotes reconciliation. In this way the mimetic impulse harbors our deepest humanity, and our deepest freedom. Against God, abstract truth, and the anti-Semite stands the reflective–humanistic–mimetic impulse guarding real freedom, preserving meaningful–reconciled freedom. "It is against this freedom that the idiosyncratic aversion, the purported motive of anti-Semitism, is ultimately directed." (151)

In other words the idiosyncratic aversion is an unreflective instrumental tool. It maintains its proximity and lack of reflection, so that anti-Semites, although they detest Jews, are driven to "imitate them constantly."(151) By imitating the Other, unreflective people can have their cake and eat it too. By imitating others who are different they get the enjoyment of mimesis combined with the power of instrumental domination. In other words, they use others by mimicking them. Through this instrumental imitation of the Other they are able to harken back to a time of surviving through assimilation, without having to admit this "weakness". There is a freedom in letting oneself go, in dissolving the self into something else through imitation. So anti-Semites, like racists, imitate others so they can enjoy the assimilation without admitting the fact and without giving up the instrumental advantage. Today, in America, this is all too common.

Racism is not a simple matter. It has a history and entanglement in the dialectic that defies any simple categorization. This is why so many are confused when Donald Sterling is called a racist. He hired black coaches and black athletes and owned a team in a league made up of 80% African American athletes. So how can he be a racist? Dismissing or reducing Sterling's racist comments to Sterling's eccentricity shows the absurdity of the idiosyncratic defense. For the appeal to idiosyncrasy prevents reflection on what it really going on. Reflection might show that Sterling both envies and detests African Americans.[1] On the one hand, he grants them this mythical power. He thinks they are physically and spiritually better suited, "made superior," for playing basketball. He has a mythic belief that the African American athlete is sanctioned by the gods to dribble a basketball. Ironically, he is reluctant to hire white players, as the white player lacks that *je ne sais quoi* of the darker athlete. On the other hand, he also views African Americans as inferior. He has a vague sense that they will corrupt his elite (elite only from his standpoint) white culture and his pristine (pristine only from his standpoint) female companions. There is just something about the African American that unsettles him. So he really doesn't want African Americans to be seen on the same level as him, he doesn't consider them equals, and he doesn't want them associating with his women. The anti-Semite always needed and longed for the Jew, as the racist needs and longs for the black man.

Everyone knows our world still has racism, but it's interpreted in various ways. Many whites agree there is racism today but they may also think it

---

1 This connection came to me thanks to John Ganim's excellent lecture "The Middle Ages and Its Others," CHASS Distinguished Research Lecture, Riverside, CA, April 30, 2014.

is racism directed at whites. It is not uncommon for Caucasians to think whites are at a disadvantage in our society. When the dominant group thinks they are victims, they need to be very careful and ask if this belief is protecting them from looking inward, from analyzing themselves. Perhaps it is not that they are at a disadvantage, but perhaps it is that their "whiteness" occupies so much of the American lifeworld that the smallest change to this totality creates a misperception and misinterpretation. Perhaps it is like anti-Semitism.

Ultimately, though, race is an ideological distraction hidden as an idiosyncratic aversion. Seeing the world through race, as too many do, is a type of blindness. It's an instrumental tool used to promote and protect particular and unholy interests. Rather than fruitful conversations on race we have silly banter over the use of the "n" word. In this debate some whites become idiots and ask: "why can they use the word and we can't?" Conveniently forgotten is the fact that words have different meanings in different contexts. We all use language differently in different situations, and it doesn't follow that just because one person or one group can use a word that therefore everyone can use that word. What we say to our children or spouse, the pet names that we use, etc., are words that it's appropriate for us to use but not necessarily for another, not someone outside the family. No one else should be calling your wife by the same affectionate names you call her by. So when someone asks, "why can they use the word and we can't?" they are being willfully ignorant.

In the case of the n-word, African Americans can use the word with each other because they are internally linked to it; they should control the term, and set the conditions for its use. Within the group, sometimes it's used to communicate solidarity, sometimes anger, and sometimes it's just a habit, a pre-reflective turn of phrase. Still, everyone should be careful with this word. Those African Americans who defend the use of the word can become stupid, too, when they try to be too clever. When people make a distinction between the "e" and the "a" versions of the word, they are outwitting themselves. Both versions carry regressive meaning. And to try to split them with pseudointellectual banter reveals a lack of reflection and exposes a rationalization concealing a lack of responsibility.

In the "Notes and Sketches" section of DE, there is a profound piece called "against knowingness" which articulates a lesson of the Hitler period warning of "the stupidity of cleverness."(173) The point here is that we need to be careful about outwitting ourselves. There were many expert arguments by Jewish intellectuals "proving" that fascism was impossible in the West. "Clever people have always made things easy for barbarians, because they are so stupid."(173) As our world becomes more and more clever and statistically savvy, we are allowing for more and more stupidity. Whether it is the clever arguments that rationalize use of the "n" word, the clever arguments on the benefits of climate change, the clever arguments on how sports builds character, the clever arguments justifying why evil is not God's fault, and so on, the point remains that true enlightenment is against this type of "knowingness."

The knowingness that *DE* is critiquing stems from blindness in the ideology of hegemonic instrumental reason. This ideology sees the world abstractly and through a lens which views the Other but doesn't see the Other, for it sees the Other as an object in its world and never as a subject with its own needs, interests, and points of view. In part, this is expected because the dominant group is the eye of authority. It is the gaze that the rest of society must abide by. It can validate or it can objectify. The power of the eye fears the power of what it cannot control. This is true even on a basic biological level.

One thing sight cannot completely control is smell. The nose and its ability to smell is like an Other for dominant, objectifying sight. For in smell the "nostalgia for what is lower lives on, the longing for immediate union with surrounding nature." (151) Smelling's power comes from its ability to attract without objectifying, and in so doing reveals "most sensuously the urge to lose oneself in identification with the Other." (151) Smell, "as both the perception and the perceived—which are one in the act of olfaction—is more expressive than other senses. When we see we remain who we are, when we smell we are absorbed entirely." (151) In our world, smell is more often regarded as something degrading. Since smell cannot be easily suppressed like other acts of mimesis, smell gets put to instrumental exploitation. It's more common to hear someone criticizing how someone or something smells than it is to hear someone praising a new or unique odor. Making fun of other people's odors makes it easy to forget the beauty that is possible through this sense. "Civilized" people learn not to smell. Except for the ability to sniff out bad smells, civilization largely ignores this sense. But without the ability to smell, the sense of taste gets distorted. Smell and taste are interrelated. Like smell, taste absorbs us. As people lose the ability to taste and appreciate real food, you see a loss of the intrinsic enjoyment of food. Food turns into a vulgar commodity as even the senses learn to desire the non-food we call the American diet. For our senses are not ahistorical givens; they change over time. They are a part of our contingent and human history. As Marx put it: "The forming of the five senses is a labour of the entire history of the world down to the present."[1] When a Big Mac is more

---

1 Karl Marx, *Economic and Philosophic Manuscripts of 1844*, the Marx-Engels Reader (New York: Norton, 1978) 88-89.

desired than fresh fruit, something has gone horribly wrong. When people accept high fructose corn syrup in most of their food, and fake, processed cheese covering their plates, we have absorption without human sense. Without the ability to sense and mimic rationally, we lose touch with part of our deep, living, and better selves. As we lose the power of our senses and power over our senses, more and more of the concrete human self gives way to abstract and manipulated pseudo-subjectivity. Only in a culture without robust taste and smell could people fall in love over the internet.

Quinoa

Still, human horizons are always shifting, and what appears foggy today might become clearer tomorrow. As our horizon shifts, so does our sense of self. Even our senses dialectically yearn for our best selves, and they can help us discover and perhaps rediscover hidden segments of existence. For example, on the horizon today a new way of feeding ourselves, a new way of overcoming alienation in terms of food consumption is perhaps emerging in mass consciousness. The irrationality of our food culture is coming into focus. Perhaps the rationality of non-processed foods, or whole foods, or a plant-based diet is coming into focus. Most of food history has been a struggle with nature to overcome scarcity. Having enough to eat was a gift of fortune and not a given. Modernity has conquered food scarcity and yet we have outwitted ourselves with our enlightened processed success. Still, if we listen carefully, the Sirens' song may be heard and take the form of a mythic memory of food before factory farming, before high fructose corn syrup, before "freedom fries." Americans, for the most part, have lost the taste of "natural," clean, healthy food. The fast food industry manipulates this memory and leaves us impotent and obese. Is it rational or moral to consume factory farmed meat, eggs, and milk? Is processed food unambiguously an advance in civilization? The particular interests of the food industry (like ancient priests) work tirelessly to assure that we consume in this unholy manner. But perhaps we are sacrificing and renouncing a better part of ourselves when we accept the given of today's diet. Food should be intrinsically enjoyable and instrumentally healthy. Maybe rejecting processed foods and unethical factory farming is a step toward reconciliation. Can one seriously go through the McDonald's drive through with "not of this world" plastered on the back window? Does a Carl Jr.'s commercial invoke reconciliation with beauty or barbarism?

As cunning becomes second nature, we see over and over how we have outwitted ourselves. Today with nearly 50% of Americans grossly overweight and diabetes at an all-time high, we've outwitted and outfitted ourselves. DE warns us that when humans cut themselves off from the consciousness of themselves as nature, the noble purposes for which they keep themselves alive can quickly become void. The quest for self-preservation can destroy the very thing which is to be preserved until we are only left with preservatives. But we must always be reflective. Veganism is the new fad, the new commodity, working its way through the American commodified intestine. With phony baloney, hipster vegan restaurants, vegetarian celebrity books, and so on, money and power quickly become the focus for this industry. And it's also becoming a religion. We have all met "born-again" vegans and these new vegans are linking their food habits with the metaphysical urge, turning it into a religion, and fetishizing it. "The Sacred Church of the Quinoa" is the last thing we need.

Through the Looking Glass

But the sense that *DE* is most concerned with is perception. Perception is a tricky business. Perception is intimately connected to the dialectic since it is the foundation of the gaze. Although seemingly straightforward, perception is not something immediate or simply given. Rather perception involves mediation and interpretation from the start. Human perception is biological, historical, conceptual, and imaginative. There is always already understanding, evaluating, and judging within the act of human perception itself. With all this going on language becomes central to perception.

Language, as we saw earlier, allows a tree to be more than a tree; allows us to see the Other as more than another. When enlightenment has reached a stage in which the rational use of mimesis has become taboo, then perception and the language that accompanies it redirects the mimetic excess in a manner that keeps the enlightenment ideology intact. Modern self-perception affects perception so that we perceive in the Other aspects of ourselves that we cannot admit come from ourselves. The aspects we have repressed, in the name of self-preservation, might seem as something outside us in the same way that excess from perceiving a tree might seem like mana from heaven. This is complicated by the fact that a tree is never a tree anyway. As Sartre has taught us, we carve up the world and create the differentiations we supposedly find in the world. The world just is, it's an in-itself, and it's we who bring nothingness, meaning, and value to the world. The realization and the nausea it incites, like the cry of terror, has phenomenological implications. A tree can be more than a tree because a tree is never really or merely a tree. Likewise, the Other can be more than another because the Other is never really or merely other. To think the Other is completely other is a false projection. False projection is easiest to see in anti-Semitism.

"Anti-Semitism is based on false projection." (154) False projection is the reverse of genuine mimesis in that if mimesis makes itself like its surroundings, false projection makes its surroundings like itself. The external world, from the standpoint of mimesis, is the standard to which the self attempts to adhere, while with false projection the self is the standard to which the external world must adhere. But what is especially problematic here is the loss of truth in distorted projection. It is false, meaning that this self which makes the world conform to itself does so from the standpoint of ignorance. This self projects itself into the world and makes the world resemble itself, but all the while it does not recognize or admit this fact. This is very dangerous because "Impulses which are not acknowledged by the subject and yet are his, are attributed to the object: the prospective victim."(154) Others are prospective victims here because they are seen as something they really are not. They are accused of something they have not done and so cannot defend themselves. In some cases others may get credit for good things they haven't done, or for that which they don't really represent, but in most cases what is attributed to the outside is something negative. For the person who projects falsely is suffering from a sort of sickness, and so sees sickness in the world and in others. Further, in a wrong society, the wrongness of the society will not be acknowledged by the society as its own wrongness, rather this wrongness will be projected into others, both individuals and other societies. Again, the obvious example here is the Nazis' projection of fascist traits into Jews. The sick person or sick society sees sickness only in the Other. Ted Cruz's irrational attack on The Affordable Care Act exemplifies false projection. This sort of projection is "both a ruse and a compulsion." (154) The disorder of false projection "lies in the subject's faulty distinction between his own contribution to the projected material and that of others." (154)

When George Zimmerman targeted Trayvon Martin, he clearly was making a false projection. From all indications Trayvon was not doing anything wrong. Zimmerman projected his own fears of crime, projected from the problems they had in the neighborhood, and had internalized an irrational and instrumental manner for dealing with his fears. Not a policeman, yet playing one, Zimmerman created a world and a situation in the image he already perceived the world as being, and he created the tragic outcome. While Zimmerman was under the spell of false projection, Martin was under the spell of immature and child-like mimesis. Martin had apparently bought into the regressive and mythic gangsta style and the violence that often accompanies it. This macho and violent ideology kicked in when pursued by the stranger Zimmerman. We see here that when stupid and false projection meets violent and immature mimesis, nothing good will result.

We all have a bit of Zimmerman and Trayvon in us. "In a certain sense, all perception is projection."(154) We project our needs and wants into the world in order to satisfy those needs and wants. Sometimes these correspond to the reality of the object and sometimes they don't. And as historical creatures our needs and wants change over time. The projection of sense impressions has a long history going back to animal history. It is a mechanism that aids in obtaining food, in defense, a readiness for combat that advanced animals seem to need and to continually develop. Much of this occurs and evolves regardless of the intention of the object. By the time we get to human history, projection is highly automated and much of it is geared toward survival. As conscious creatures we can reflect on this and on ourselves. Language can be a help and a hindrance, a trap and a means for emancipation. In our history we have had to fight, scratch, and adapt to survive, so self-preservation colors much of human perception. Yet if civilization is to advance, we must learn to control projection: refine, inhibit, and reflect on it. Early on as children we learn to distinguish our thoughts and feelings from others, and the very idea and recognition of a distinction between inner and outer, both within oneself and between others, develops. And "the possibility of detachment and of identification, self-consciousness and conscience" (155) grows. Through self-reflection, through determinate negation of the given, we can continue to cultivate and create our best selves. This is a dialectical and creative process that, as moderns, we can embrace.

From *DE*'s perspective, Schopenhauer, better than Kant, understood and articulated that the perceptual image does indeed contain concepts and judgments from the very start. Perception is not just a reflection, guided by the intellect, of data received from real objects by the brain that is then ordered by the mind. Rather, "between inner and outer, yawns an abyss which the subject must bridge at its own peril. To reflect the thing as it is, the subject must give back to it more than it receives from it." (155) Perception is an active act of creation in which the subject is forced to work from the smidgens that the senses have brought in, and from these pieces the subject can begin to recreate experience, and in this way create the world. We learn to give unity to the traces of things that we take in, and from this model we create a self and build a unified self in the same manner. But just like the outside world, this creation and recreation, comes after the event. In other words, the self only gets constituted retroactively in piecemeal fashion from within an ever-swirling abyss. In this way we can say that the modern self is a "unified and, at the same time, an eccentric function." (155)

If the self is constituted on the model of external perception, and if the material for the self comes from the world and must be forged retroactively from traces, then the inner depth of a person is nothing other than "the delicacy and richness of the outer perceptual world." (156) But this outer perceptual world is always being formed and reformed from our experiences and our conceptual understanding. When we stop "seeing" or stop thinking, the self is in danger of petrifying. Against this sort of immediacy, "only mediation can overcome the isolation which ails the whole of nature." (156) Rejecting isolation through mediation, through self-reflection, creates the "possibility of reconciliation."(156) Cultivating meaning, understood as making sense of one's life, while maintaining mediation, is human enlightenment; it is reflection guided by reason, a reason that is conscious of its own projection.

What makes perception false, then, is denying one's projection. When we deny what we bring to perception, we become pathic. "Because the subject is unable to return to the object what it has received from it, it is not enriched but impoverished."(156) This impoverishment can quickly move from a false projection into paranoia. "Because paranoiacs perceive the outside world only in so far as it corresponds to their blind purposes, they can only endlessly repeat their own self, which has been alienated from them as an abstract mania." (157) Paranoiacs grab whatever is within reach, miss its uniqueness and peculiarity, and shove it into their mythic sack of a self. Paranoiacs feel all-powerful, but that is only because they have created a closed circle, an echo chamber, that is mistaken for the world. This chamber repeats endlessly their monotonous self. Like the Christian God who purportedly needs no one but insists that everyone worship him, paranoiacs put themselves at the center of the universe and, in a narcissistic version of the metaphysical urge, relate everything back to themselves and insist that their "system knows of no gaps." (157) Therefore what false projection ends in is calamity.

Daft Punk[1]

The only cure is philosophy. As we saw above, perception is only possible "in so far as the thing is already apprehended as determinate." (160) Dialectical philosophy analyzes the determinate, knowing that it is only determinate because the subject is projecting into the object, the subject, through mediation, is creating the differentiations. Philosophy slows perception down and as "thought identifies the conceptual moments which are immediately posited in perception and are therefore compelling, it progressively takes them back into the subject and strips them of their intuitive power." (160) Philosophy takes the self through the stages of what

---

1 Apologies to the Dead Kennedys and authentic punk.

seemed obvious and shows its contingent, historical construction. In this way philosophy throws off the curse of the metaphysical urge and the search for absolutes. "The subject which naively postulates absolutes, no matter how universally active it may be, is sick, passively succumbing to the dazzlement of false immediacy."(160) Against this sickness, philosophy recognizes itself as a creation and not merely as process of discovery. Philosophy doesn't posit absolutes; rather it seeks to reconcile the particular and universal in a never-ending human construction.

But even philosophy must be especially careful, because a judgment that doesn't postulate absolutes but stresses its contribution must still assert its own content as something not merely individual and subjective, because judgment itself is a claim to truth and "Truth, unlike probability, has no gradations."(160) Further, the reflection beyond the individual judgment, the ability to negate the judgment, must also take itself for the truth. This contradiction rescues truth, but also contains a paranoid moment, since it is distrustful of its own initial judgment. This is what makes all reflective thought somewhat paranoid, and is actually what determinate negation requires: a critical–paranoid reflection aware of itself. Ironically: "Paranoia is the shadow of cognition." (161) Yet awareness of the moment of paranoia and the act of rationally transcending it, negating it, breaks the spell of the reified given.

But unlike philosophical reflection, the paranoid person cannot take the negating step. The paranoid clings to the initial judgment. The paranoid is too consistent. Too much consistency is a sign of a lack of consistency in thought. Determinate negation requires following through in critiquing the absolute claim and continuing to qualify ones judgment. This is difficult though: "For reflection, which in the healthy subject breaks the power of immediacy, is never as compelling as the illusion it dispels." (161)

We are not wired up to reflect on our judgments until, perhaps, they run into the reality principle. That's why so many find philosophy annoying. In a weird way philosophy threatens our survival, for during "the formative period of the human sensorium those individuals survived in whom the power of the projective mechanism extended most deeply into their rudimentary logical faculties, or was least moderated by the premature onset of reflection." (161) Even today, science generally shuts down thought at a point designated by social need, and this is why one can say science is constantly in danger of just becoming a slave to technology. Of course it's not just science; the ability to know when to reflect and when to act is important in most spheres of life. An athlete who "thinks too much" is in danger of losing his or her ability to play well. The last thing you want to do at the free throw line is reflect. Rather, you want to shut down thought, relax, and let the mechanics and the muscle memory take over; you just want to shoot the ball. Yet, before you get to the free throw line, if you want success, you better have practiced, and practiced reflectively and deliberately, for hours upon hours. Successfully maneuvering through this dialectic of thinking and acting is an art. As art, as philosophy, one must reflect on one's judgments and on the structure underlying these judgments. This is the value of philosophy for society. When critical reflection gives way to false projection, it must be called into account, whether one finds it annoying or not. This is why Horkheimer and Adorno's philosophy goes back to the origin of religion.

For the origin of religion is one of misinterpreting the world and a misperception of the materiality of our world. It projects the subject's fear into nature and transposes nature into something spiritual. This origin makes religion materialist down to its marrow. For religion was a misinterpretation of material reality and has never delinked from craving and taking power in society. From this skeleton it creates, sometimes unknowingly perhaps, a childlike, false, affirmative notion of reconciliation. And as we saw earlier the culture industry mimics and manipulates this logic and copies the power grab of spirit. In this way both religion and culture are not spirit, they are not un-dialectically the superstructure. They are material, they are base. Not in a mechanistic sense but in a dialectical sense, in which materialism means a human social practice. As social practices they are not abstract ideas, rather they are concrete, determinate forces. For they actually exist because of us, hold institutional power, and both are driven by economics and defined by class structure. Just as myth and enlightenment are intertwined, the mode of production in our world is drenched in the exchange value of these seemingly innocuous industries.

Religion, then, occupies a peculiar space in the history and realm of false projection. In individuals and peoples it endlessly repeats itself as farce. Religion began as a misinterpretation of nature and about nature, and so began as a mistaken way to achieve self-preservation. Worshipping supernatural beings does not affect how nature operates. But religion gained the power of self-preservation when others accepted religion and granted power to those claiming to understand it. So while religion cannot aid in preserving oneself from nature it does aid one in cultural survival. Whereas science actually can aid in self-preservation and, because of its tremendous success, threatens to destroy culture, religious projection destroys both the truth of nature and the truth of culture. The religious mind is a paranoid mind that projects God into everything. It is "the symptom of the half-educated." (161)

In true dialectical fashion then religion fights and exacerbates paranoia. For paranoia, as a neurosis, is an individual sickness. Neuroses are asocial formations that individuals struggle with. But when a specific type of false projection becomes a group projection, it takes on a social formation, a social status, and doesn't develop as a neurosis. In fact, this specific false projection, this sickness, is a social advantage as the "paranoid mechanism is made controllable, without losing the power to strike terror. Perhaps that was one of the major contributions of religions to the survival of the species." (162-3) Members of a religion can relieve their paranoia by participating in the approved group form of delusion. Go into any mega-church today for a firsthand look at this.

One of the great accomplishments of modernity was to push back against religious paranoia and develop rationalist and empiricist modes of enlightenment. In the choice between a supernatural and a natural explanation, greater humanity made the right choice in opting for the later. But losing one's religion turned into the commodification of culture, as the eternal soul gave way to the reified–commodified self. The price paid is that the "present order of life allows the self no scope to draw intellectual or spiritual conclusions. Thought, stripped down to knowledge, is neutralized, harnessed merely to qualifying its practitioner for specific labor markets and heightening the commodity value of the personality. In this way the self-reflection of the mind, which counteracts paranoia, is disabled." (163) Yet, we are lucky, it's not disabled as *Dialectic of Enlightenment* shook off the metaphysical urge, seized enlightenment as script, and prepared humanity for "a positive concept of enlightenment which liberates it from its entanglement in blind domination." (xviii) So whether we heard it from a coach or Seneca, we know that "luck is what happens when preparation meets opportunity," and, as Daft Punk put it for our age, it's time to get lucky[1].

---

1 Getting Lucky is not really about "hooking up". It's about making a connection and creating meaning. See: http://popdust.com/2013/04/22/daft-punk-pharrell-get-lucky-lyrics-meaning/ and http://blogs.villagevoice.com/music/2013/09/nile_rodgers_get_lucky.php

Excursus. A Novel Dialectic

Modernity is vast, it's wide and deep, and the virus named wrong society has not colonized or corrupted all of it. The novel, as an art form, pushes back against wrong society for it lives on reflection and grows with self-reflective readers. Perhaps the condition of possibility for "novel" reading, for language—not song, is slowness, reflection, and, at least implicitly, an anti-metaphysical urge. And as we saw with the *DE*'s reading of *The Odyssey*, a "novelesque" sensibility, the awareness that dialectics is best understood as determinate negation, allows for the uncovering of latent, hibernating human truth. By analyzing the rise of the novel in modernity and reading it as script we can further consider questions of meaning and reconciliation within modernity. In life and in literature, meaning is that which allows individuals to make sense out of their lives and reconciliation occurs when that sense links up to the sense the community has of the significance of human life. We will begin with literature.

Milan Kundera links the modern age to the rise of the novel, to the conceptual idea of the novel form through history. On the one hand, Kundera sees modernity as a time that has robbed human life of meaning; on the other hand, he argues that the novel form holds on to meaning in a kind of hibernation. As Kundera sees it, the modern world is a trap. In the first place, the "wideness of the world" that "used to provide a constant possibility of escape"[1] no longer does so. In this regard, World War I was the decisive event. A European war, it is aptly called a world war because it signaled that really no event on our planet is merely a local one. We find ourselves more and more under the control of external forces, in inescapable situations, and becoming more and more alike. Second, as moderns,

---

1 Milan Kundera, *The Art of the Novel* (New York: HarperPerennial, 2000) 27. All future page numbers from Kundera will be in the text and designated with a "K".

we are conscious that life is a trap, for we realize that "we are born without having asked to be, locked in a body we never chose, and destined to die." (K 26-7) The modern world is a disenchanted one. Following Heidegger, Kundera argues that as our world became more and more specialized, we lost sight of the world in its totality and lost sight of our own selves. For both Heidegger and Kundera, the modern world is guilty of "the forgetting of being." Kundera poetically tells us in slow language: "As God slowly departed from the seat whence he had directed the universe and its order of values, distinguished good from evil, and endowed each thing with meaning, Don Quixote set forth from his house into a world he could no longer recognize. In the absence of the Supreme Judge, the world suddenly appeared in its fearsome ambiguity; the single divine Truth decomposed into myriad relative truths parceled out by men. Thus was born the world of the Modern Era, and with it the novel, the image and model of that world." (K 6)

In dialectical fashion then Kundera locates the creation of the novel with the rise of a non-metaphysical modernity, and he reads the vicissitudes of modernity through the lens of the novel. One could say that he sees the novel as a model for determinate negation as "the novel" takes it upon itself to investigate our "forgotten being," and to scrutinize concrete life. Unlike traditional philosophy, which searches for abstract and certain truth, "true" novels see the world as ambiguous and have only "the wisdom of uncertainty" as their certainty. (6-7) Thus while some see the novel's purpose in edification and others view it in merely aesthetic terms, Kundera says: "The sole raison d'être of a novel is to discover what only the novel can discover. A novel that does not discover a hitherto unknown segment of existence is immoral. Knowledge is the novel's only morality." (5-6) The novel cannot be captured in a position, be it moral, political, or aesthetic for it is, at its core, an inquiry. The novel's language is one of relativity and ambiguity. Its wisdom is that of uncertainty and of the essential contingency of things human. In this way it upholds the deepest values, the positive values, of a non-metaphysical enlightenment.

Yet, if the novel is predicated on uncertainty and ambiguity, then perhaps the era of the novel is coming to an end. Like Horkheimer and Adorno, Kundera claims our disenchanted, scientific minds have trouble seeing uncertainty and ambiguity. The novel cannot survive today because the novel's spirit is one of complexity, it constantly reminds us that: "Things are not as simple as you think." (K 18) But if we are witnessing the death of the novel, it will also be the death of the modern era and the problem of modernity won't be a problem. Not because we solved the problem of modernity but because our novelesque sensibility, our self-reflective being, like the Dodo bird, has gone extinct. For according to Kundera what is killing the novel is the rise of a "totalitarian universe." (K 14) Kundera means by this not something political or moral but rather ontological. The modern world, like the novel, represents a time of hope, doubt, and questioning that is now fading. Kundera's artful articulation of the death of the novel mirrors *DE*'s claim that "enlightenment is totalitarian." But even in a totalitarian universe, the dialectic ensures that we will have spaces to grow if we know how and where to look. And as historical creatures, who keep trying to shrug off the metaphysical urge, who embrace enlightened modernity, we need to look at ourselves both individually and collectively. It is worth repeating Habermas's trenchant phrase reminding us that "Modernity can and will no longer borrow the criteria by which it takes it orientation from the models supplied by another epoch; *it has to create its normativity out of itself.* Modernity sees itself cast back upon itself without any possibility of escape."[1]

We cannot escape modernity but we also are not simply trapped in modernity. Freedom within aspects of our world ensures that we can challenge actual existing modernity from the inside, dialectically, of course. A novelesque or dialectical approach then is possible within modernity from those schooled in its art. And there's no one better at this art than Horkheimer and Adorno's contemporary Georg Lukács. For Lukács's version of determinate negation not only centers on the novel like Kundera, but it also, like Horkheimer and Adorno, contrasts modern society with the ancient world of Homer.

More Than Literature

According to Lukács, in Homer's pre-capitalist society the practices and institutions of society at large legitimated normative beliefs, and so in that sense meaning was directly given. As Lukács eloquently begins *The Theory of the Novel*: "Happy are those ages when the starry sky is the map of all possible paths—ages whose paths are illuminated by the light of the stars...the fire that burns in the soul is of the same essential nature as the stars...each action of the soul becomes meaningful and rounded in this duality: complete in meaning".[2]

According to Lukács, it is in these ages that epics can be written. The theme of a Homeric epic is not simply about personal destiny but rather speaks to the destiny of a community. The point is not that there were no individuals in the Greek world but rather that individuals in the age of the epic are integral components of their societies. Homeric heroes cannot

---

1 Jürgen Habermas, *The Philosophical Discourse of Modernity*, Frederick Lawrence, tr. (Cambridge: The MIT Press, 1992) 7.
2 Georg Lukács, *The Theory of the Novel* (Cambridge: The MIT Press, 1999) 29. All future citations to Lukács will be within the text and designated with an "L".

conceive of themselves independently of their community and so their fate cannot be disconnected from the fate of the community. In these "integrated civilizations" meaning is already written into empirical experience, and right and custom are identical with morality. The ancient epic expresses the form of totalized cultures. These "integrated civilizations" are closed circles in which harmony exists between individual selves and the world. There is an acceptance of values so the destiny of the epic hero is never personal but rather it signifies the destiny of a community. As Lukács puts it: "each action of the soul becomes meaningful and rounded...complete in meaning...and draws a closed circumference round itself." (L 29) Further, "the epic hero, as bearer of his destiny, is not lonely, for this destiny connects him by indissoluble threads to the community whose fate is crystallised in his own." (L 67)

Lukács recognizes that this lack of alienation rests on an unfree relationship between individual and community and on the underdevelopment of individuals. But his point is that "the mind's attitude within such a home is a passively visionary acceptance of ready-made, ever-present meaning. The world of meaning can be grasped, it can be taken in at a glance; all that is necessary is to find the *locus* that has been pre-destined for each individual." (L 32) In this sense it is a homogeneous world. There is reconciliation of subject and object and subject and subject.

In fact the initial vision for *The Theory of the Novel* "was meant to take the form of a series of dialogues." (L 11) These conversations were to have a Platonic feel in that they were to involve a group of young people as "they try to understand themselves and one another by means of conversations." (L 12) Through the conversations, the path of enlightenment could emerge despite being caught, and somewhat trapped, within what Lukács calls "the Dostoevskian world." (L 12) Lukács's dialectical approach then captures the ambiguity of Plato's version of the metaphysical urge. Plato's use of conversations, of interlocutors, is consistent with a novelesque approach and yet his Platonism, his escape into a world of Forms, undermines the approach. In this way we can say the progress and decline of modernity also goes back to our first great philosopher.

These contradictions persist into the writing of Lukács's *The Theory of the Novel*. Writing near the conclusion of World War I and grateful for the outcome in which Western civilization was saving us, Lukács also saw that the question arising from it was "who was to save us from Western civilization?" (L 11) So a book on the theory of the novel is really a book about much more than that. *The Theory of the Novel* is not simply a quest to understand how to theorize the novel, but rather it is the quest to understand modern life for "the problems of the novel form are here the mirror-image of a world gone out of joint."(L 17)

Lukács begins his analysis by positing the dualism between an integrated and what he calls a "problematic civilization." By examining the question of the epic through this lens, he implicitly adapts a dialectical framework. The negative dialectical moment is captured in the ancient world that serves as a guilty conscious for our current problematic civilization. While contemporary civilization is fragmented, the epic arises from an integrated civilization. Integrated civilizations might be happy but they are not mature; they correspond to Hegel's first stage of history in which there is undifferentiated harmony. The metaphorical stars are the universals open to individuals at their historical time. Perhaps it's not even correct to call them individuals (at least not in the modern sense) but in any case the point is that the path of the person is already formed from tradition and authority. The world one finds oneself in internally sets the limits and defines the vision of one's individual life. In this way Lukács can say everything is "new and yet familiar." (L 29) The world and the self are separate but not separate. They are separate in that the world is bigger and seeming more important than the individual. It came first and exerts a power over the individual. Yet they come from the same substance, share the same goals, they exist in the same home. Meaning comes from this duality, for individual and society form a "rounded" or complete circle.

Philosophy arises when this completeness is challenged or where it might break apart. "This is why the happy ages have no philosophy, or why (it comes to the same thing) all men in such ages are philosophers, sharing the utopian aim of every philosophy." (L 29) For we all start out as creatures of the epic, so to speak. We have no interior life until we have external experiences in which to fill the inside. But in integrated societies the external is not seen or felt as external, so there is a feeling of completeness within and without. "The soul goes out to seek adventure; it lives through adventures, but it does not know the real torment of seeking and the real danger of finding." (L 30) This soul is too immature, too young to know that it can lose itself or that it can even look for itself. This is what it means to live in the age of the epic.

It is not that individuals do not feel suffering or worry about self-preservation, rather "it is the adequacy of the deeds to the soul's inner demand for greatness, for unfolding, for wholeness" (L 30) that holds individual and society in harmony. The soul does not know any abyss within itself that might coax it to jump or to "discover pathless heights," for it is like father to child when the child only longs to be like the father and "every action is only a well-fitting garment for the world. Being and destiny, adventure and accomplishment, life and essence are then identical concepts." (L 30)

The question of the epic, then, is "how can life become essence?" Homer is the master here, for he answered the question before anyone had explicitly asked the question. This is part of the beauty of the Greek world; it was a world that had answers even before people explicitly started to ask the questions. It's a world of dialectics without dialectical thought. The integrated ancient world organically unified individual life with Greek essence, so the questions never arose. Questions arise when problems arise, when one gets pulled short, when there are anomalies and counterintuitive experiences. So when life and essence were one, Homer could show what it meant before anyone wondered what it meant. It's like enjoying a good film, one you have seen before, and celebrating the moving and entertaining scenes a second or third time even though you already know the ending. It is new in so far as the individual has gained new interests, desires, and ideas that draw out previously missed or ignored parts and still it is familiar in so far as it continues to connect the individual to his or her past and his or her life. Yet in the Homeric Age, no new "film" genres emerge, and no new endings get introduced, as this age can bring happiness but not maturity; and so it falls short of modernity's potential.

For Lukács to say that the Greeks had answers before they had questions is to say that their problems were of a quantitative, not a qualitative, nature. It was a question of whether one could accomplish one's task, a task defined from the outside, perhaps prior to the individual or from above. Because of this, rather than facing something insurmountable, something "which cannot be bridged except by a leap" (L 32) the individual feels up to the task, for it seems as something placed there for them. In this way "the mind's attitude within such a home is a passively visionary acceptance of ready-made, ever-present meaning. The world of meaning can be grasped, it can be taken in at a glance" and one must just find what one's destiny is, what has already been predetermined just needs to be discovered. One only commits an error if they give too much or too little, "only a failure of measure or insight" is possible. Knowledge comes from seeing what is there but hidden, knowledge as creation is "only the copying of visible and eternal essences, virtue a perfect knowledge of the paths; and what is alien to meaning is so only because its distance from meaning is too great." (L 32)

This is a world before subjectivity, in the modern sense, as even the "soul stands in the midst of the world." It is homogeneous so that the differences of the soul are not different in essence from other things. The lines are drawn for the purpose of a homogenous system to maintain its balance. It is a pre-Cartesian world where the individual is not a unique or elevated substance. The individual stands below the family and the state even as this individual is intimately part of family and state. All elements are on the same road. So although the road may be long, and the journey home long, there is no abyss to surmount and no desire for an abyss.

In this closed world external and incomprehensible forces may be felt, but not so strongly as to "displace the presence of meaning; they can destroy life, but never tamper with being." (L 33) The modern self that *DE* is defending against enlightenment distortion cannot breathe in a closed world like the Greeks. For in the modern age, "we have invented the productivity of the spirit" and with it we have lost the world that the Greeks saw as self-evident. By inventing new forms we feel incomplete. And we have "found the only true substance within ourselves." (L 34) Our thoughts and actions split until we have even created an abyss between "us and our own selves." (L 34) Our world is bigger, with greater rewards and greater dangers, "but such wealth cancels out the positive meaning—the totality—upon which their life was based." (L 34) The Greek totality was one of a world in which something closed could also be complete. There was nothing pointing to anything higher. By reaching one's highest, one submits to limitation—but limitation within a pre-given homogeneous world. These limits are not seen as limits but are felt as reconciliation and experienced as consciousness realizing itself by realizing its predetermined fate. As such it brings to the surface of this world and the form of this world an understanding that "knowledge is virtue and virtue is happiness, where beauty is the meaning of the world made visible." (L 34) Today we are in danger of losing this beauty of the ancient Greek world and, at the same time, losing the freedom to transcend through modern subjectivity. Thus we need to look more closely at the transition from Homeric song to Platonic philosophy so as not to forget this aspect of "being" that has been bequeathed to us.

The question that Homer answered before it became a question finally becomes an explicit question, and it becomes visible with the emergence of Greek philosophy. Ironically only when Homer's world is ending does his world become conscious enough to actualize and to articulate philosophically; Hegel's owl of Minerva flies by. The stages of epic, tragedy, and philosophy provide grist for the mill that Lukács utilizes creatively to analyze questions of literature and life simultaneously. If the epic answers the question of "how can life become essential?" by expressing the unity of the particular and the universal, then the stage of tragedy can be read as a response to the falseness of this answer. Tragedy asks "how can essence come alive?" This second question emerges because the first question becomes problematic. Human life comes to feel the trap of a pre-given, reified essence. For this pre-given essence reduces the particular to almost an epiphenomenon as it is ultimately essentially unnecessary for the essence. The tragic hero pushes back against this lack of differentiation. Rather than trying to make one's life essential one tries to make essence come into concrete life through the journey of a lonely, tragic hero.

Still a "paradox attaches to loneliness in drama. Loneliness is the very essence of tragedy, for the soul that has attained itself through its destiny can have brothers among the stars, but never an earthly companion; yet the dramatic form of expression—the dialogue—presupposes, if it is to be many-voiced, truly dialogical, dramatic, a high degree of communion among these solitaries." (L 45) The language of the lonely is monological as "loneliness has to become a problem unto itself" as the soul attempts to overcome the problem of tragedy. The truly lonely soul is not simply "gripped by destiny" "it is also the torment of a creature condemned to solitude and devoured by a longing for community." (L 45) This type of loneliness gives rise to new problems, like those of trust. Without trust the individual dives deeper into the self and, as any good Hegelian knows, quantity may transform into quality, until the selves' deep individual thought transforms into philosophical cognition.

But as soon as the tragic hero makes this qualitative move to philosophy, philosophical reflection, with its analytic tools, further separates what is the case from what ought to be the case. The tragic hero begins to question what this essence really is and if it's really worth it to live a lonely existence in the name of an idea. The philosophical question becomes one of asking what the point of trying to maintain immanence is. This is the beginning of the critique of the metaphysical urge. We see Plato torn within his own soul as he struggles to cast off the metaphysical urge and at the same time redefine it. The character of Socrates holds this in dialectical tension. The Socrates of the *Apology* casts off the urge as the Socrates of the *Euthyphro* clings to it. Within Plato's articulation of Socratic philosophy the answer to the question of tragedy reveals itself as but a "cruel and senseless arbitrariness of the empirical, the hero's passion as earth-bound and his self-accomplishment merely as the limitation of the contingent subject, did tragedy's answer to the question of life and essence appear no longer as natural and self-evident but as a miracle, a slender yet firm rainbow bridging bottomless depths." (L 35-6)

Life is more than any essence can capture. Life is richer than gods and more complicated than geometry so closed circles cannot sustain in reality. As the circle inevitably fragments and breaks, the harmony of the epic gives way to tragic resistance, and then to philosophy's nihilism. But Plato couldn't swallow the bitter pill of nihilism and created a new harmony with his theory of Forms, only to be supersized with Christianity. Plato wanted happiness and maturity, and heroically he went down fighting for both. He could be refuted but his legacy only cured. But with no antidote in sight his

Christian legacy insisted on making the world round again as it invented "a totality capable of being taken in at a glance" (L 37) and with it "aesthetics became metaphysics once more" (L 38) But to make this move is to "forget that art is only one sphere among many, and that the very disintegration and inadequacy of the world is the pre-condition for the existence of art and its becoming conscious." (L 38) In this act of forgetting then, Christianity regressed to infantile happiness and unwittingly proved history is not teleological, and eschatology is but a bad joke. But some bad jokes keep being told even though no one is laughing. For sometimes the silence seems worse. It's taken centuries for the silence to settle in us, but it finally has settled, like a nuclear winter, snowing down on modernity.

Our wintery world, our world without external foundations, forces maturity but not necessarily happiness. Many then deny this history or rationalize Kant's attempt to avoid it. Yet it is clear we have no secure stars in modernity, for cognition works at night, and "to be a man in the new world is to be solitary." (L 36) As solitary one's inner light only illuminates the next step. Subjects are not objects to themselves. They cannot tell if their actions match their essence. For we cannot "glimpse the bottom of those depths" and without this insight art becomes independent, it stops trying to copy reality, for it realizes it must create its own totality, "for the natural unity of the metaphysical sphere has been destroyed forever." (L 37) This, it seems, is too much for most people to accept. It's a road less traveled as many still would rather vacation to the familiar, even if it has lost the magic it once contained. Even if the familiar location has been destroyed the urge to visit is not destroyed so quickly or so easily, and self-deception has its day again; recommence genuflection.

The Road

This brings us to the stark contrast between epic and novel and the maturity that is only possible with a novelesque sensibility. "The novel is the epic of an age in which the extensive totality of life is no longer directly given, in which the immanence of meaning in life has become a problem, yet which still thinks in terms of totality." (L 56) In the novel, the hero is a seeker. "The simple fact of seeking implies that neither the goals nor the way leading to them can be directly given." (L 60) "The epic hero is, strictly speaking, never an individual." (L 66) His destiny represents the destiny of a community. He is not lonely "for this destiny connects him by indissoluble threads to the community whose fate is crystallised in his own." (L 67) In Dante "we see the architectural clearly conquering the organic" (L 68); and so we see a transition from epic toward novel. Dante's hero need not be a king or socially superior and his destiny need not be co-determined with that of the community. For "his hero's lived experience was the symbolic unity of human destiny in general." (L 69)

"The novel is the art-form of virile maturity, in contrast to the normative childlikeness of the epic." (L 71) The novel's completeness shows an imperfect world and "if subjectively experienced, it amounts to resignation." (L 71) Self-recognition sometimes takes the form of irony. "The irony of the novel is the self-correction of the world's fragility...everything is seen as many-sided, within which things appear as isolated and yet connected, as full of value and yet totally devoid of it, as abstract fragments and as concrete autonomous life, as flowering and as decaying, as the inflection of suffering and as suffering itself." (L 75)

When the melancholy hits, it hits in the way Sartre explains the death of God. The mature response to the overcoming of the metaphysical urge is one that "thinks it very distressing that God does not exist, because all possibility of finding values in a heaven of ideas disappears along with Him; there can no longer be an *a priori* Good, since there is no infinite and perfect consciousness to think it."[1] Sartre's maturity is clear for he recognizes that in this world, meaning is still sought, a novelesque sensibility is maintained. As Lukács puts it: "The novel is the epic of a world that has been abandoned by God." (L 88) Maturity, though, does not mean proud, dry, seriousness. In fact, those who elevate themselves and their existence to replace God, Sartre calls "stinkers"—for they cannot acknowledge the true consequences of the death of God and cannot tolerate a post-metaphysical world.[2] Anyone forced to drive the highways around Los Angeles surely has encountered their share of stinkers. Stinkers or not, they misread the implications of the death of God by elevating themselves to a deity. Like those who can't handle the implications of our human condition and so reach for pre-mature reconciliation in Cormac McCarthy's *The Road*, and in so doing distort his slow, beautiful ending because they inject a Christian conclusion into the final pages. The final paragraph of this novel stresses the beauty of the human spirit, as well as what most will cling to in dark times, even as it also reminds us we are part of nature, and what we do and who we are, for better or worse, will remain part of the World's never ending becoming. Perhaps how one understands the last pages of this hauntingly sublime work is a Rorschach test for how deeply the metaphysical urge resides within one.

In any case, the modern world, as a world abandoned by God, still contains the psychotic. This world hides God in different locations like a children's game of hide-and-seek. The various forms of the novel give us clues to where this God is hiding. Lukács says there are roughly two places to look

---

1 Jean-Paul Sartre, *Existentialism and Human Emotions* (New York: Citadel Press, 1985) 22.
2 Ibid., 46.

for the incommensurability of the particular and the universal in modernity: "either the world is narrower or it is broader than the outside world assigned to it." (L 97) These two places that capture the incommensurability have only grown today, but not only through novel forms. They have grown in the lifeworld, through things like religion, as pre-modern art forms have replaced the modern novel form.

The first form is "abstract idealism." With abstract idealism there is a "demonism of the narrowing of the soul," but this is hard initially to see, for the problem presents itself as a problem of an outward failure rather than an inner emptiness. Because the soul is so narrow the abstract idea, although without substance, becomes the only thing worth worshipping. Encapsulated in an individual or character, abstract idealism takes on a hyper-reality that cannot accept that reality cannot match the individual's big idea. These individuals think that because their idea should be, it must be, and that since reality doesn't satisfy the idea "reality is bewitched by evil demons and that the spell can be broken and reality can be redeemed either by finding a magic password or by courageously fighting the evil forces." (L 97) These sorts judge all of reality from within a narrow soul that imprisons their soul in a mental safe-house until it becomes incapable of experiencing anything at all. In this safe-house actions are "spontaneous and ideological at the same time." (L 100) This imprisonment, this isolation, makes the soul resemble a work of art but also separates it from the external world and even from other parts of the self which have not "been seized by the demon." (L 100) The robust inner meaning creates a correspondingly robust "senselessness and the sublime turns to madness, to monomania." (L 100) Today this takes shape in contemporary life forms that define themselves against modernity. They reject modern knowledge in favor of petrified ancient texts or abstract ideas like faith. The abstract idealist needs the corrupt external world to fight against. More than the inner soul sustaining the self, one relies on the profane external world to give one's beliefs substance, even if only negatively. This "abstract idealist" has split today into two main types. The first is the dangerous, barbaric terrorists blowing things up to "honor" their prophet. The second blends within the lifeworld as a conservative and respectable citizen hiding its true regressive, empty nature. There is a boogey man behind every door and a cultural battle to fight against the secular society. Bill O'Reilly's "culture warriors" are always at war and so never have to face the reality of their emptiness. There's always a war on Christmas, so to speak, thus there's never a moment to cultivate a conciliatory self. O'Reilly, like Mrs. Jellyby in Dickens's *Bleak House*, lets his abstract obsessions fill his soul while right under his feet sleeps flea-infested Fox News. In short, abstract idealists project into their empty selves a wicked outer world to fill themselves with, because, paradoxically, without the profane or liberal outside, they have nothing and are nothing.

Although alive and well today, these narrow souls came into being at a time when the paradox of the Christian universe could first be felt. It migrated from Dante to Descartes, so that by Descartes's time it could be used ideologically and strategically by the philosopher (see *Meditation* I). This world is one in which God can still fruitfully be accepted and, at the same time, be conceived of as an evil demon, a *deus deceptor*. From the literature side, both Kundera and Lukács pinpoint *Don Quixote* as the moment that brought into consciousness: "the beginning of the time when the Christian God began to forsake the world; when man became lonely and could find meaning and substance only in his own soul, whose home was nowhere." (L 103) Rather than acknowledging this truth, religion ignores it and like Don Quixote continues to fight windmills. Still, against this petrified metaphysical urge, we see here the potential for a new human totality. This potential is the potential to grasp a true totality. A true totality is not imaginary or totalitarian but rather is one that sees the human contribution to the world, and sees the higher dialectical possibilities that were always possible from the first creative act of differentiation. With this insight, the realization that "what makes the whole truly a whole is, in the end, only the effective experience of a common basis of life and the recognition that this experience corresponds to the essence of life as lived at that moment." (L 109)

On the other side of the incommensurability, in a world abandoned by God, stands the disillusioned romantic. Both the abstract idealist and disillusioned romantic thrive today because they are faith-based. In a global capitalist world, faith has replaced knowledge[1] so that these types have only become more totalitarian since Lukács's time. Faith-based religions, religions not rooted in robust culture, are flexible puppets for global capitalism and the manipulation that naturally follows from lack of roots. But whereas the abstract idealist is without content and so needs the external world to avoid emptiness, the disillusioned romantic avoids modernity for his own inner and fuller reality. The disillusioned romantic has a soul that is as "wider and larger than the destinies which life has to offer it." (L 112) The inside "is like a cosmos, it is self-sufficient." (L 112) Romantic disillusionment takes the form of trying to avoid conflict and struggles; it is passive. The external world is seen as meaningless and so not worth struggling over. Modernity is just a bad, old world to be ignored. The inner reality, the preference for this psychological structure, is also a value judgment on reality. This structure rejects the notion of utopia. "Life becomes a work of literature; but, as a result,

---

1 Olivier Roy, *Holy Ignorance* (New York: Cambridge University Press, 2010).

man becomes the author of his own life and at the same time the observer of that life as a created work of art." (L 118) "Everything that happens may be meaningless, fragmentary and sad, but it is always irradiated by hope or memory. And hope here is not an abstract artifact, isolated from life.... it is part of life; it tries to conquer life by embracing and adorning it, yet is repulsed by life again and again. And memory transforms the continual struggle into a process which is full of mystery and interest and yet is tied with indestructible threads to the present, the unexplained instant...the moment of failure is the moment of value." (L 126)

The beauty of Lukács's analysis shows that these novel forms can be read to represent reality and, at the same time, offer critical resolutions. In the novel form the ideology is grounded into the form of the text, into the materiality, so that the ideology is not floating helplessly, because the structure of the text is providing grounding. That is why some of the problems of life are not problems of literature. In literature one can contradict life, one can transcend life's contingency, and one can achieve limitlessness. In this way it's not incorrect to say that sometimes literature is more dialectically-materially rooted than our actual world. Contrasting our world to a text we can see that the abstract idealist and romantic disillusionment, as attached to contemporary religion, have lost their root in the text, as they have lost their roots in culture and society. As such the virtue of religion loses its way or gets squeezed out of the religion. What remains of the "religious text" then looks at best more like a fragmented text, and at worst, an ignorant commodity. The soul of religion, emptied of its spiritual content in globalized modernity, has been pushed into a forced choice of either defining itself against modern culture (like the abstract idealist) or entirely breaking from the larger culture (like the disillusioned romantic).

In either case, the "progress of modernity" has made religion more "pure" as it delinks from any particular culture, place, or lifeworld. The result has been that today's thriving religions, more or less, view modern culture as a threat and an enemy. For the religious mind modern culture has the reputation for being materialistic, vulgar, money-hungry, and perhaps even pornographic. But, at the same time, religion acts like any other commodity and actually embraces a type of nomadism. Religions pride themselves today on not being rooted. One is not limited to living in Utah to sustain a Mormon identity, nor must one travel east to become a Buddhist.[1] With globalization, religion becomes more fundamentalist because fundamentalist religions accept and perhaps insist on this break with culture and place. With this break, fundamentalist religion can feel unique since it is more pure and, at the same time, it can pitch itself as universal since it is willing to

1 Ibid.

go anywhere. It circulates outside of knowledge and culture in a special "knowledge free zone" that grants it special privileges within the modern world. It pitches itself as mysterious and as simple and as absolute. It is the highest articulation of the metaphysical urge today.

And like any modern commodity, one need not labor much to satisfy this contemporary metaphysical desire. Today one can become religious, become "born again," or get converted in less time than it takes to buy a car, and certainly in much less time than it takes to read a good novel. Structurally though, today, procuring a religion is much more like buying a car. In fact the logic is pretty much the same. Americans have a love affair with cars. Watch any car commercial and it's loaded with images of sex and power, seducing the viewer closer and closer to his or her relationship with the automobile. Becoming a car owner or converting to a new make or model is a metaphysical experience. It all begins with dissatisfaction or a sense of meaninglessness, an unhappiness or fear because the car one is driving is just not satisfying. Or maybe one doesn't even own a car (God forbid, in America), so one begins to search. The pilgrimage might take the path of browsing the internet, visiting dealerships, taking test-drives, talking to friends, listening to car shows, and dreaming of sitting in a Lincoln, next to the prophet Matthew McConaughey, during all the car commercials throughout the big game. At some point, though, one must choose, one must take a leap of faith. The hardest part is dealing with the dealership, the half a day wasted as you negotiate. As the salesman checks with his boss, checks with finance, and tries to bamboozle you into a lease rather than a purchase, the clock keeps ticking. Still, there's nothing like that new car smell in which to baptize the self as one pulls off the lot.

And so it goes today with religion. The beginning is a feeling of dissatisfaction, loss of meaning, fear. And probably a struggle with an addiction, be it alcohol, drugs, sex, shopping, or any number of addictions plaguing America today. In any case, one begins to search via the web, or by visiting churches, or perhaps talking to friends, or getting approached at Starbucks or even your home, until it culminates in a choice. Choosing one's religion then allows for a trip to the church, a quick lying on of hands, or a splash of water, or a quick prayer, and you are off the lot. Converted, born-again, with that new God feeling soaking into the pores as you leave the church, you can blast the Christian rock through the surround-sound speakers. As you begin your atomistic relationship with God, you can simultaneously drive home alone in your car of choice; finding Jesus or Lexus is just splitting hairs. After this you can throw away the books, the thinking, the agony, and just live on faith and fill up on gasoline. The more faith, the less one needs or wants knowledge, the less reason one has to read good novels. For where there is faith, there is no need for knowledge.

The religions that survive in our knowledge-free, instrumental world are the ones that offer the slickest advertising or simplest messages. Christian Pentecostalism and Mormonism are among the fastest growing religions for obvious structural reasons. Speaking in tongues, speaking without language, is the ultimate dream of the metaphysical urge. If one can access the urge without language, human intelligence gets bypassed. Without language dialectics is impossible and critical thought is transcended. The emperor-God has no clothes but no one has the words to say it. This is why Oliver Roy can say, without hyperbole, we are witnessing the age of "holy ignorance."

As religion relies more and more on faith and less and less on knowledge, it dovetails with the death of the novel. A totalitarian universe banishes knowledge and novels for the mythic mantra of the faithful and the unambiguous. But where enlightenment rationality, linked with the science faithful, allows the scientist to walk proud in contemporary society as the new priests, the religious faithful must keep their heads down in the modern world as they ponder their unhappy choice: ignore the profane, larger culture or fight against it. Either choice though reveals that religion is vacuous or incoherent without the profane. It either willfully ignores contemporary knowledge and lives anachronistically across the street hidden in some tract home of American society or it embraces crazily and proudly a pre-modern politics that pushes for a return to America's (of course mythical) religious roots. The isolated ones keep their children away from larger culture, keep good novels out of the house, and live as shadows. The obnoxious side tries to transform culture to suit their beliefs and to attract the next generation. Both sides have a difficult task since religion and culture have split irreparably. Without culture to ground it faith has to do more work than it's suited for. For how can one pass on their beliefs when all they have to draw on is personal feelings or mere inner perception? Faith is a private concept that one accepts or rejects outside of cognition. Evidence is not to the point. The religious one, whether trying to ignore or transform culture, ends up just aping culture. To attract the next generation religion today mimics youth culture. But, of course, youth culture is not really culture. It's just the latest fads and marketing gimmicks. Still you see more and more churches falling for it as today's new ministers spend their lives trying to look hip and up-to-date. They wear jeans, have stylish haircuts, are on Facebook and Twitter, they play Christian rock. There is a flood of Christian movies from *Heaven is for Real* to *God Is Not Dead* that don't realize they are kooky, and unwitting parodies of bad Hollywood films. To the holy, they are engaging works of art.

Try Not To Take A Knee

Despite the false representations of truth in both abstract idealism and romantic disillusionment, Lukács, like Horkheimer and Adorno, did not give up on the positive conception and potential of enlightenment. Lukács articulates that positive side by showing how Wilhelm Meister moves beyond the contrast of abstract idealism and romantic disillusionment. Reading Wilhelm Meister can serve as an apprenticeship for those lost in the sea of holy ignorance. For its "theme is the reconciliation of the problematic individual, guided by his lived experience of the ideal, with concrete social reality." (L 132) The interiority in this text stands between idealism and romanticism. Community here "is the fruit of a rich and enriching resignation, the crowning of a process of education, a maturity attained by struggle and effort. The content of such maturity is an ideal of free humanity which comprehends and affirms the structures of social life as necessary forms of human community, yet, at the same time, only sees them as an occasion for the active expression of the essential life substance." (L 133) This goes beyond "rigid political and legal being-for-themselves" so that the heroism of abstract idealism and the pure interiority of romanticism are justified "but only as tendencies to be surmounted and integrated in the interiorized order." (L 134)

Lukács stresses that art is not life and that art simply helps us see ourselves and our world. It helps us uncover new ways of being but cannot replace life or literally transform us. For "art can never be the agent of such a transformation" "any attempt to depict the utopian as existent can only end in destroying the form, not in creating reality." (L 152) In Lukács's time, the new novel form emerging was made concrete through Dostoevsky, and Lukács recognized that it signaled an emerging new world. But it seemed a radical break to Lukács. A break deep enough that he could say "Dostoevsky did not write novels," for Dostoevsky "belongs to the new world." (L 152) Like Horkheimer and Adorno, Lukács was grappling with this new world and he knew that, with the change in the structure of the novel, the question becomes whether we are "about to leave the age of absolute sinfulness or whether the new has no other herald but our hopes." (L 153)

Living in the age of Tebowing, suffering through the age of holy ignorance, this question has been answered in a way that unfortunately validates Horkheimer and Adorno's pessimistic side. Yet history keeps marching on, it continues to become, and now we can ask another, related question: Does the age of Tebowing signal the ending of the metaphysical urge or the repetition of farce?

We saw above that beginning with the idea of an integrated and homogeneous civilization Lukács is not suggesting that we go back to such a time but rather he treats it dialectically to expose the problematic nature of our differentiated and heterogeneous modern world. Our world is the world of the novel, and the "novel is the epic of a world that has been abandoned by God." (L 88) What this means, according to Lukács, is that novel writing issues from a world in which forms of intelligibility and meaning are no longer directly given; not authorized by tradition or community. The result is a turn inward toward subjectivity, a look to ourselves: "the outside world is no longer adapted to the individual's ideas and the ideas become subjective facts—*ideals*—in his soul." (L 78) This is Kundera's point before Kundera made the point.

According to Lukács, the novel is unique because of the way its form leads it both to accept and to reject the exile of values and meaning into subjectivity.[1] Unlike the epic, the novel cannot rely on antecedently validated value assumptions. The novel "is the epic of an age in which the extensive totality of life is no longer directly given, in which the immanence of meaning in life has become a problem, yet which still thinks in terms of totality." (L 56) Thus having epic aspirations, the novel must represent the social world. It has mimetic ambitions and so must represent the objective world as devoid of values and as meaningless; but in so far as it is a literary work it must give form, meaning, and unity to what it represents. As Lukács puts it: "the objectivity of the novel is the mature man's knowledge that meaning can never quite penetrate reality, but that, without meaning, reality would disintegrate into the nothingness of inessentiality." (L 88) Aesthetic form in the novel stands in for the value assumptions and beliefs of past narratives. In other words, the novel's literary form is where values and meaning reside when they are exiled from the social world and cast into subjectivity. This is just a Hegelian way of making Kundera's point that the novel demystifies the metaphysical urge, rejects a leap into "true reality," and sees that conceptualization was always dialectical from the start. The novel is an enquiry into what it means to be human without skyhooks dangling above us.

J. M. Bernstein articulates Lukács's point by arguing that novels can be read dialectically in terms of form giving (making sense of a subject's life) and mimesis (reflecting the world we live in).[2] In other words, the novel must represent the modern condition in order for the text to be intelligible at all. At the same time the text forms a coherent whole (even if only negatively) and goes beyond mere representation to offer interpretation and to suggest meaning. These two moments of the novel correspond to the Kantian worlds

---

1 J. M. Bernstein, *The Philosophy of the Novel* (Minneapolis: University of Minnesota Press 1984).
2 Ibid.

of causality and freedom, of is and ought.[1] The dialectic of the novel is the attempt to capture the world as it is in terms of how it ought to be. The novel is premised by the gap between is and ought, between what Lukács calls, reification and self-recognition, between mimesis and form-giving.

Through this dialectic the novel gives us a sense of how modern subjects are split within themselves. As we saw earlier one side of this split Lukács labels the "empirical subject." Here one finds him or herself lost in a meaningless world. This is the experience of alienation or reification. Still, another part of us, the "transcendental subject," combats this by articulating "a new and autonomous life that is, however paradoxically, complete in itself and immanently meaningful: the life of the problematic individual." (L 78) The problematic individual, or reflective individual, strives to make sense of his or her life even at the cost of self-preservation. This transcendental subject is essentially a free self, but is unable to determine the world because our world lacks reconciliation. The problematic individual, though, need not fall victim to a petrified modernity, but rather, like the novel form, can create human meaning through a dialectical synthesis of form and content, of particular and universal. This enlightened, modern self can create human meaning as he or she learns to transcend mere self-preservation, the metaphysical urge, and instrumental reason. A free modern self will not sacrifice self-reflection, human community, or intrinsic values; this modern self will not simply take a knee.

Lukács's argument concerning the novel then offers a novel solution to the problem of modernity. Following Bernstein we can say the novel's narrative captures the dualism of Kant's epistemology and at the same time the novel employs normative standards that allow for a more critical resolution. Kant does not try to unify phenomenon and noumenon, nor can he posit substantial values given his formal definition of reason. Rather Kant insists that there are things-in-themselves which we have no access to, and he takes self-reflection out of reason. Against Kant, the novel sees lack of unification as a problem and attempts to solve it; the novel posits substantial values because it frees subjects and communities from metaphysical tutelage. In a world without God we still have each other; and, as Richard Rorty famously said, we need to "keep the conversation going" or, as Habermas puts it, engage in communicative discourse. Conversations among individuals, communities, and through texts doesn't guarantee meaning or reconciliation, but it beats a world where people think they can transcend the wants and needs of others because of a "conversation" with a supernatural entity. The novel form structurally points to true representations of the dialectic or as Lukács was fond of saying: "Art always says 'And yet!' to life." (L 72)

---

1 Ibid.

Horkheimer and Adorno are often accused of having no answer to the problem of modernity. But refusing to accept false notions of meaning and reconciliation should not be mistaken for lack of answers. Determinate negation, despite the pessimistic tone, is a way of saying "Yes to life." Even in the bleak times they lived through, they gave us tools to see possibilities beyond the given. By taking an instrumental world and transposing it into a novel form, the *DE* kept human meaning and human knowledge in hibernation. As such they were able to represent a world without meaning, a world with meaning imposed from above, and still they were able to supersede it. Determinate negation shows there are other possible meanings to our lives and it reminds us that if we forget this, if we forget how to maturely narrate our lives, we will be unable to create the meaning and find the reconciliation possible in modernity.

Dialectics, kept alive in the form of the novel, explains how the modern self has lost some of its connection to community and some of its subjectivity. Still, as novelesque, the modern self can combat the alienation and fragmentation of a capitalist society by projecting a rich, many-sided image of human wholeness. The novel form cannot stop at or completely accept the abandonment of meaning and reconciliation. The novel captures the desire to unite form and life, and achieve meaning and reconciliation. What this means Lukács explains: "[T]he creative subjectivity glimpses a unified world in the mutual relativity of elements essentially alien to one another, and gives form to this world." (L 75)

Horkheimer and Adorno, then, like Lukács, would agree with Kundera that it is no accident that the novel is the most characteristic art form capable of challenging a reified modernity. The novel is abstract and mirrors the contemporary world. Unlike the epic hero, the hero of the novel is a lonely, isolated, problematic individual who experiences homelessness in a fragmented world. Homelessness, in an alienated world, is a mark of maturity. The homeless one has lost faith in the old foundations and has lost substantial ties to other individuals and the world. The objective world is emptied of meaning and value and although the objective world is a human product it becomes reified as a "second nature." The novel represents this reified world and by giving form to it points towards its overcoming.

Horkheimer and Adorno, Kundera, and Lukács all push back against abstract enlightenment logic by appealing to dialectics, to the novel. Modernity, with its emphasis on instrumental reason, is less and less able to see, as Kundera puts it, "the world as a whole" and finally suffers "the forgetting of being." (K 3-4) This continues until "Man has now become a mere thing to the forces (of technology, of politics, of history) that bypass him, surpass him, possess him. To those forces, man's concrete being, his 'world of life' (*die Lebenswelt*), has neither value nor interest: it is eclipsed, forgotten from the start." (K 4) Despite the Heideggarian jargon in Kundera, this push back against the "forgetting of being" is push back against the metaphysical urge. Instead of simply reading from the Big Book, we need to read many good books, for if we don't push back in the name of concrete human freedom, we will never understand the abstract, sinister logic of capitalism or the irrational, religious blowback playing out across the globe today.

Appendix. Sport As Enlightenment

Sports are, of course, instrumental. The goal is usually to win the game, score the goal, cross the finish line first etc. But are strategy and winning really the driving forces of sport or does something else ground our interest in sports? Perhaps the instrumental aspects of sports are secondary to the human meanings and understanding that we strive for when we play sports. Usually only one team or individual wins, but despite this most people who play sports enjoy themselves. And it's not just organized sports: during recess, at the park, in the recreation center, and so on, we see people competing, training, and working out by themselves and with others. How many individuals still look back at their high school, college, or playground games as some of the fondest memories of their youth? How many athletes continue to want to play their sport even after their bodies are unable to perform at the same level or even though the team clearly is not going to win a championship? The instrumental aspects of sport are secondary to the intrinsic and meaning-creating aspects. This sometimes gets forgotten; sport is rooted in community and the desire for individual transcendence.

The ideas of community and the longing to express the individual's concrete being are, of course, not only found in sports. They also thrive through most activities, including philosophy. In fact these values were central to the philosophy of critical theory starting with Karl Marx. Marx's vision for an enlightened modernity is surprisingly simple, like most sports, and achievable for more than one "team." This sort of success, success that balances the intrinsic and instrumental, is a choice and a matter of will. This sort of success envisions a world that refuses to let the metaphysical urge trump human needs and human interests. It stands for a world that takes the values of freedom and equality seriously by refusing class society and rejecting private control of capital. It is in Marx's articulation of a successful modernity that the positive side of enlightenment, that *DE* prepared us for, lives.

Adorno says somewhere that we shouldn't just look for the old in the new but that we should also look for the new in the old. In that spirit I want to take another look at Marx to see if his vision of a successful modernity, his break with the metaphysical urge through his rejection of Hegel's Absolute Spirit, produced a concrete alternative for analyzing and resolving the new problems that Horkheimer and Adorno grapple with in regards to domination, labor, and ultimately meaning. It may not be incorrect to say that Marx was concerned with enlightened sport; his focus was on concrete, human practices, both individually and collectively, rather than with the activity of an Absolute Subject. Yet the sport of philosophy has grown since his time, and we don't want to ignore the progress critical theory has made. So we will look at the old and the new, at Marx and at Habermas, as sport.

Frances (Ha)bermas

Marx wants to keep practice and labor as central moments for actualizing the project of modernity. The critical theory tradition, and especially Habermas, has moved away from this emphasis. In the case of Habermas, it would be a mistake and a misreading to think of him as a Frances Ha, who's going to find a way to make it in New York, so to speak, even if he doesn't have the aesthetic qualities of someone like Adorno. Habermas has been criticized for not having the radical flare of his predecessors. It's a tricky business trying to make it in the wake of the first generation critical theorists. From the trenchant critique of "one dimensional man" by Marcuse, to the radical–spiritual insights into "the age of mechanical reproduction" of Benjamin, to the aesthetic critique of the "culture industry" by Adorno and Horkheimer, the first generation seemed to be stars on Broadway. In contrast, the dense and analytical style of Habermas can seem rather dreary, even where it is extremely difficult and complex. But like the film *Frances Ha* one only has to look at little deeper to see how radical and unorthodox Habermas's critique is. For underneath the film's romantic comedy look and underneath Habermas's dense style sits radical brilliance and daring theory. The former deconstructs the Hollywood formula and the later does the same to the "philosophy of consciousness."

Habermas begins with the seemingly innocuous claim that modernity is "an unfinished project."[1] Habermas calls for critical theory to make a paradigm shift from the "philosophy of consciousness" to one based on

---

1 Habermas (1992).

communication.[1] Habermas calls this paradigm shift "communicative action." This means that philosophy should abandon the model of an individual subject confronting an object as theoretically central and replace it with an intersubjective model based on language. According to Habermas "The focus of investigation thereby shifts from cognitive-instrumental rationality to communicative rationality."[2] What defines communicative action "is not the relation of a solitary subject to something in the objective world that can be represented and manipulated, but the intersubjective relation that speaking and acting subjects take up when they come to an understanding with one another about something."[3] Emphasized with this move are intersubjectivity, language, and concepts such as validity and consensus.

According to Habermas, the problems for the critical theory tradition stem from their adherence to the model of the philosophy of consciousness. Subject centered philosophy, with its subject/object dualism, is naturally suited to instrumental rationality. Demystifying nature so it is no longer godlike easily transformed to seeing nature as a tool to be used and manipulated for strategic human purposes. As we have seen, the dialectic of enlightenment that Adorno and Horkheimer trace shows this. In other words, the philosophy of consciousness with its subject/object dualism has real difficulty transcending instrumental reason. Thus, what begins in Kant and Hegel as a positive reading of the powers and capacities of reason turns, with Horkheimer and Adorno, into a negative one. The end result, according to Habermas, is that this tradition has taught us that "the paradigm of the knowledge of objects has to be replaced by the paradigm of mutual understanding between subjects capable of speech and action."[4] With this paradigm shift should come insights into the possibility for actualizing the potential of modernity.

Communicative action then puts the linguistically mediated relations among subjects at the center of its analysis.[5] This move, instead of emphasizing a subject's manipulation of objects, and defining rationality in terms of the success or failure of that manipulation, focuses on the specifically linguistic phenomena through which social relations are produced and reproduced, and defines rationality in terms of concepts such as validity and consensus. This is what is meant by the rational basis of speech.

With the move to communicative reason, then, Habermas has new tools for social theory in what he sees as a crucial distinction between system and

---

1 Vogel (1996). My interpretation of Habermas has been greatly influenced by Vogel's articulation.
2 Habermas, *The Theory of Communicative Action*, Thomas McCarthy, tr. (Boston: Beacon Press, 1984) 392.
3 Ibid., 392.
4 Ibid., 295.
5 Vogel (1996).

lifeworld.[1] The system/lifeworld distinction builds upon the communicative thesis in the sense that the forms of the lifeworld are rendered ideally as communicative. The lifeworld forms the linguistic context or background for processes of communication. Systems, in contrast, involve the economy and the state and they operate, not through communication, but instead through media of money and power, respectively. Habermas follows Weber's theory of rationalization in claiming that modern societies can be seen as becoming both more differentiated in system functions and rationalized in lifeworld functions. The system functions become more differentiated meaning that the economy and state integrate diverse activities in accordance with their respective logics (money and power) by regulating the unintended consequences of strategic action through market or bureaucratic mechanisms without relying on agents' intentions. In this way, social systems become ever more differentiated while lifeworld functions, such as socialization and the transmission of tradition, are increasingly subject to the demand for reasons. Social change is said to occur through the progressive rationalization of the lifeworld insofar as the norms and values are subject to challenge. Normal processes of rationalization within the lifeworld occur through communicative action while the modernization of the economy and state proceeds through instrumental and strategic action. The later development, driven by the motors of money and power, are healthy as long as they stay within their proper sphere. In these ways system and lifeworld continue to develop according to their respective logics. Further, they become more differentiated from one another, so that lifeworld functions are increasingly freed of the burdens of systems functions and vice versa. As they do each new system development is said to add further life possibilities.

The problem, for Habermas, comes when systems logic begins to overflow and penetrate the lifeworld. Habermas calls this phenomenon the "colonization of the lifeworld."[2] Colonization of the lifeworld is the taking over of communicative imperatives by strategic ones. As in language the communicative takes priority over the strategic, in social theory the lifeworld trumps the systems. Hence, when strategic action is primary, ordinary forms of discourse are distorted. Likewise when systems imperatives impose their weight on lifeworld ones there is a distortion of the lifeworld. The colonization of the lifeworld thesis provides Habermas with a unique perspective for critiquing both moral theory and social theory.

But we must be careful here because Habermas distinguishes system and lifeworld in a way that, unlike Marx, allows for alienated labor. First, Habermas allows for this because he is worried that if we lose the

---

1 Habermas, *The Theory of Communicative Action*, Vol. Two. Thomas McCarthy tr. (Boston: Beacon Press, 1987).
2 Ibid.

system/lifeworld distinction then instrumental logic could eat up the communicative realm. If we cannot separate out the communicative from the instrumental then we could end up back to the complete domination that worried Horkheimer and Adorno. Also if we treat labor communicatively (as opposed to materially and instrumentally) we could forfeit the advances that modern instrumental reason has given us in science and technology. We could lose the efficiency that modern labor has afforded us. As committed to the progress of modernity, Habermas wants to stress the material and instrumental aspects of labor and he is willing to live with the domination that comes with it. Habermas's theory then sees labor and production as equivalent to instrumental action. One begins to suspect that Habermas himself has fallen victim to the metaphysical urge as his worries expose a privileging of a foundational material realm in so far that he relies on an instrumental relation in the sphere of the economy to produce positive results. He seems to think there is some underlying material realm not subject to human mediation. The urge goes deeper with Habermas as he also tries to ground his theory in what he pitches as a universal and "rational basis of speech."[1]

Despite the metaphysical overtones, Habermas's worries seem legitimate and yet, from the perspective of the Hegelian-Marxist tradition, there is something disconcerting about the system/lifeworld distinction as Habermas formulates it. Specifically, from the perspective of Marx's concerns, it is troublesome that one can say so little about the modern system of labor. In fact, there seems to be an ambiguity in Habermas's paradigm shift to communicative reason that comes out when we consider the place of labor in his theory. His objection to the philosophy of consciousness is that it takes subject/object relations as primary and so ends up assimilating subject/subject relations to the former. But Habermas now gives up on subject/objects relations, ceding labor to the systems domain. So it seems that labor now threatens to drop out of critical theory's project. Habermas criticized Marx for emphasizing labor and ignoring interaction but the way Habermas sets up the system/lifeworld distinction one can ask if he is making the opposite mistake. By leaving labor to a systems logic and hence to domination Habermas seems to restrict major areas of human social experience from formation through processes based on communication.

One can posit then that from Marx's vantage point this split may make it difficult to understand the extent to which labor, as part of the system, needs to be embedded in and directed by communicative practices. Because Marx is clear about the alienation caused by focusing on labor's system aspects,

---

1 Habermas, *Justification and Application*, Ciaran p. Cronin, tr. (Cambridge: MIT Press, 1993).

he is in a better position to talk about communicative control of labor than his successors, and especially more so than Habermas. Marx's social theory emphasizes labor's capacity to give concrete expression to human projects and hence to form and actualize human ideas of the meaning and value of human life. Moreover, in doing so, the theory allows Marx to show that labor need not be domination and that a concern with giving meaning to life need not imply teleology.

According to Marx, meaning, understood as the ability of humans to make sense of their lives, originates through our laboring practices. When we seize control of our practices rather than being alienated, we will move towards a reconciliation that recognizes the human contribution in what seemed to be outside us, be it God, an object, or the Other. Marx is concerned that capitalism and religion make it difficult for humans to control and make sense of their individual and collective lives. Still, Marx saw the dialectical role that religion and capitalism play in human conceptions of meaning and reconciliation. Religion takes meaning and reconciliation seriously yet makes them otherworldly. Capitalism does not take them seriously yet demystifies the world such that one is free to pursue them in the here and now. We will begin with his critique of religion.

Ned Flanders

In critiquing religion Marx wants to retain the concern with meaning and values that religion harbors and yet to reject a teleological view of history. Instead Marx wants a self-justification without religious or metaphysical foundations, a self-creation able to create its own meaning and un-alienated being. Marx understands the objective world as a human and created one, expressing our values, and still he wants to be able to vouch for its rationality. But then the question arises as to how concretely we can do so once we get rid of a teleological understanding of history, and with it the loss of the idea of a pre-given meaning to life. Can we remove the idea of a religious or absolute metaphysical meaning from our lives and still affirm them as meaningful ones? Indeed, once we give up on a given meaning, can we even speak coherently about our lives at all when it seems reasonable to suppose that there is no way of specifying what a life amounts to—apart from the meaning that it aims for?[1]

One might ask why Marx, as a modern, bothers at all with religion. Marx sees that the creation of meaning is becoming an industrial process and he believes that religion will simply be incorporated into the process. Yet it is through religion, deconstructed through the process of determinate negation, that one can see elements of the human meaning that capitalism

1 Nehamas (1996).

mystifies and attempts to erase. Religion then, ironically, helps Marx offer a rival theory that can challenge the logic of capital. Marx, following Feuerbach, offers a critique of religion, then, not simply to refute it but also to analyze, incorporate, and indeed validate some of its utopian elements. Marx's critique of religion offers him a tool to recall human beings to their collective practices and to acknowledge the capacity of these practices to give meaningful expression to human life.

In the *Contribution to the Critique of Hegel's Philosophy of Right: Introduction*, Marx claims that "the criticism of religion has been largely completed; and the criticism of religion is the premise of all criticism...Man, who has found in the fantastic reality of heaven, where he sought a supernatural being, only his own reflection, will no longer be tempted to find only a semblance of himself—a non-human being—where he seeks and must seek his true reality."[1] Marx insists that the starting point for a critique of the problem of modernity is that "man makes religion; religion does not make man."[2] Here he emphasizes that it is human beings themselves that give value and meaning to their lives and that religion's spiritual ideas simply reflect our concrete practices, and the human desire for a meaningful existence. As we will see, Marx wants us to take this desire and actualize it through labor; labor for Marx becomes a mode of expressing human projects and human ideas of meaning. According to Marx meaning is literally a human construct; humans create meaning rather than meaning being something "out there" for us to discover. But why do we not see this? Because: "This state, this society, produce religion which is an inverted world consciousness, because they are an inverted world."[3]

Marx stresses the utopian element of religion in his famous, but often misquoted, reflections on religion. It is worth quoting at length to make the point. "Religious suffering is at the same time an expression of real suffering and a protest against real suffering. Religion is the sigh of the oppressed creature, the sentiment of a heartless world, and the soul of soulless conditions. It is the opium of the people."[4] Seen in context, Marx's famous line about religion being the opium of the people shouldn't evoke a drooling image of Ned Flanders from *The Simpsons*. Rather Marx's critique of religion is dialectically astute. Religion upholds deeper meanings and values than the strategic and instrumental modern world rewards. The problem, for Marx, is that religion gets the cause of our misery and the cause of the crisis in meaning wrong, casting the solution out of this world and out of human control. Philosophy, then, must not just demystify religion in a negative way,

1 Marx (1978), 53.
2 Ibid.
3 Ibid.
4 Ibid., 54.

but also serve to illuminate the positive aspects of religion, as it can be, to steal a Habermasian term, a "guardian" of human meaning and values. As Marx puts it: "Criticism has plucked the imaginary flowers from the chain, not in order that man shall bear the chain without caprice or consolation but so that he shall cast off the chain and pluck the living flower."[1] The point here is that the critique of religion should not lead one to relativism or nihilism; rather it should be as if one has "regained his reason; so that he will revolve about himself as his own true sun."[2] We must "unmask human self-alienation in its secular form" and "establish the truth of this world."[3]

"Establishing the truth of this world" is not a theoretical project for Marx. Rather it is a conscious and active practice. In arguing that we need to see that we have made religion Marx is also stressing a larger epistemological point concerning the need to see how we express and create ourselves as historical creatures. For Marx, there is no dualistic separation between humans and the world, rather we are always already in the world and always already forming and transforming it and us. The second thesis on Feuerbach states: "The question whether objective truth can be attributed to human thinking is not a question of theory but is a practical question. Man must prove the truth, that is, the reality and power, the this-sidedness of his thinking in practice. The dispute over the reality or non-reality of thinking which is isolated from practice is a purely scholastic question."[4] To say that it is through our concrete practices that we "prove the truth" is not to argue for a typical materialism that seeks to uncover what is real beneath our theories. Rather it is to deny that there is anything "underneath" to uncover. In the first thesis on Feuerbach Marx says Feuerbach too has not grasped the active, Hegelian element of practice. "The chief defect of all hitherto existing materialism—that of Feuerbach included—is that the thing, reality, sensuousness, is conceived only in the form of the object or *contemplation*, but not as *human sensuous activity, practice*, not subjectively."[5] According to Marx, "human sensuous activity" means getting beyond subject/object dualism and grasping "the significance of 'revolutionary,' of practical-critical, activity."[6] Our laboring practices are what give expression to human projects and ultimately determine the meaning of our lives. According to this argument what we do, how we express ourselves, what concrete mark we make ultimately accounts for who we are. Further, reconciliation will not happen by letting oneself go and surrendering mythically, nor will it occur

1 Ibid.
2 Ibid.
3 Ibid.
4 Ibid., 144.
5 Ibid., 107.
6 Ibid.

by instrumentally dominating. Reconciliation will be a process or concrete practice that has overcome the irrationality of an alienating metaphysics. Overcoming irrationality requires activity, "human sensuous activity." While engaged in human sensuous activity, dualisms like subject/object and human/nature dissolve and true human enlightenment appears.

Nietzsche, in discussing the ancient Greeks, makes the same point. As Nietzsche puts it:

> When one speaks of humanity, the idea is fundamental that this is something which separates and distinguishes man from nature. In reality, however, there is no such separation: "natural" qualities and those called truly "human" are inseparably grown together. Man, in his highest and noblest capacities, is wholly nature and embodies its uncanny dual character. Those of his abilities which are terrifying and considered inhuman may even be the fertile soil out of which alone all humanity can grow in impulse, deed, and work.[1]

Both Nietzsche and Marx, in different idioms, are pushing back against the metaphysical urge and prompting us to face our humanity from both sides of the dialectic. In the case of Marx the central issue is the alienation that occurs when we forget the meaning and truth of our humanity. In this sense one can say that Marx rejects the very notion of the metaphysical urge which he sees as the result of an epistemological and ontological mistake about the human condition. This break with the metaphysical urge within Marx's philosophy allows us to consider the ways enlightenment thought allows for the possibility of making sense of our lives and achieving reconciliation with others and the world. In this way Marx links directly to DE as he gives us a more concrete answer for developing the progressive side of enlightenment.

For instance, in the *Communist Manifesto*, even as harshly as Marx attacks capital, he just as strongly praises it: "The bourgeoisie...has accomplished wonders far surpassing Egyptian pyramids, Roman aqueducts, and Gothic cathedrals; it has conducted expeditions that put in the shade all former Exoduses of nations and crusades."[2] Further, all throughout the *Manifesto* what strikes us is that Marx, who supposedly hates capitalism, is not so concerned with the material objects that the bourgeoisie creates; rather, he is taken with the processes and meanings and expressions of modern human existence. He is more taken by the aesthetic, creative process.[3] The irony Marx sees is that the bourgeoisie's activity closes itself off from its richest possibilities. The bourgeoisie only really care about making money and

1 Nietzsche, *The Portable Nietzsche*, Walter Kaufmann, tr. (New York: Penguin Books, 1982) 32.
2 Marx (1978), 476.
3 Marshall Berman, *Adventures in Marxism*. (London: Verso, 1999).

accumulating capital. "It has resolved personal worth into exchange value, and in place of the numberless indefeasible chartered freedoms, has set up that single, unconscionable freedom—free trade."[1] Despite this nihilistic focus, the bourgeoisie is the first ruling class whose authority is not based on blind tradition but rather concretely on what they do. This foundation opens up new images and paradigms for an enlightened modernity. The bourgeoisie have proved that it really is possible through organized, concerted action, to change the world. Again, ironically, they cannot really admit this since it would open up new possibilities that could bury them and that, of course, Marx hopes will do so. "What the bourgeoisie, therefore, produces, above all, is its own grave-diggers."[2]

Further, in the *Manifesto*, we get additional evidence that part of overcoming alienation is showing that what seems otherworldly and static is really historical and fluid. "The bourgeoisie has stripped of its halo every occupation hitherto honored and looked up to with reverent awe."[3] Again, ironically, the bourgeoisie have made change and progress the constant embedded in the everyday workings of the modern economy. This permanent change and the relentless competition encourage creation: "The bourgeoisie cannot exist without constantly revolutionizing the instruments of production, and thereby the relations of production, and with them the whole relations of society."[4] This enduring revolution produces new types of subjects that are fluid and open like their society. As subjectivity adapts to change and even seeks change potential for both progress and decline arise. So while Marx rails against the capitalist economy, he sees potential in the personality structure it has produced.[5] This modern subjectivity then has an anti-metaphysical core to it. Existing society forces people to act and interpret in new ways and Marx hopes this will lead people beyond religion and capitalism to seize their human lives and our world concretely.

Express Yourself

The project of actualizing the progressive side of modernity in a concrete way requires an analysis of labor. Marx does not view labor as essentially domination; rather he sees labor as the condition for the possibility of expressing the meaning and significance that humans give their lives. This analysis prompts Marx to make labor the central category of both his

---

1 Marx (1978), 475.
2 Ibid., 483.
3 Ibid., 476.
4 Ibid.
5 Berman.

epistemology and his social theory. We will briefly trace aspects of Marx's argument starting with the *1844 Manuscripts*.

The *Manuscripts* begin with Marx claiming, "I have deemed... the settling of accounts with Hegelian dialectic and Hegelian philosophy as a whole— to be absolutely necessary."[1] Hegel moves the question of alienation beyond religion but he is still stuck in an idealist, and hence alienating, philosophy. According to Marx, there "is a double error in Hegel"[2] that stems from Hegel's idealism and his transcendence of the human. Hegel is right to see that "wealth, state-power, etc., are...entities estranged from the *human* being;" yet the first part of Hegel's error is that he thinks "this only happens in their form as thought...They are thought-entities, and therefore merely an estrangement of *pure*, i.e., abstract, philosophical thinking."[3] Hence, Hegel can end his whole dialectic in Absolute Knowledge. The second part of Hegel's error is that he confuses objectification with alienation. Hegel saw laboring activity as necessarily involving a loss of self and a separation from the object. For Hegel, the "knowing" subject is the true subject so labor is a secondary phenomenon. Hegel concludes from this circumstance that: "only mind is the true essence of man, and the true form of mind is thinking mind, the logical, speculative mind."[4]

In contrast, Marx argues that the objectification necessary for laboring need not be alienating. In fact, for Marx, we are primarily laboring subjects and it is either incoherent or vacuous to speak of objects until we interact with or manipulate them.[5] Since we are always already interacting in the world the issue is not whether we should manipulate or not; the issue is whether our interactions are alienating or not. Labor, rather than *a priori* being an act of destruction of something pure that alters the worked on thing and our so-called true selves, is actually the condition for knowing and creating objects and selves. Labor, seen as a philosophical concept, explodes the subject/object paradigm and shows subjects and objects are always related. First we carve up the world as a necessary condition to even experience the world. It is not that there is no world without us, rather it is that there are differentiations that we have to make for the world to be intelligible at all, these differentiations are created by mediation between us and the world. In itself the world doesn't prioritize differentiations nor does the world attribute meaning and value to existence. In this way we can say that objects do always have something of the subjective about them.[6] It

---

1 Marx (1978), 68.
2 Ibid., 110.
3 Ibid., 110.
4 Ibid., 111.
5 Steven Vogel "Marx and Alienation from Nature," in *Social Theory and Practice* Vol. 14, No. 3 Fall 1988.
6 Vogel (1996).

often begins with perception. As we saw in *DE*'s analysis, human perception constructs the world of objects based on our interests, needs, and human history. We literally differentiate the world into objects. Even subjects who are only contemplating objects and not working on them, or transforming them, are still constructing these objects through the differentiations and interpretations we must make in order to experience or contemplate an object at all. In this way objects, even those we are just reflecting on, are not really independent of us. And without us there is no reason to think objects would be constituted in exactly the same way that they are to and for us. It is doubtful that your dog or cat carves up the world exactly as you do and without any subjects it is doubtful that it would make sense of the world being carved up in any one essential way. And it is even more doubtful that it would make sense to talk about the meaning and value of the world without subjects. And even when one does posit a subject, say, God, for example, it doesn't logically follow that we would be obligated to accept or follow God's differentiations. Image how depressing it would be if you had to conform to the differentiations, meanings, and values of those who came before you, regardless of whether they were creators or not. In fact, most objects we encounter in the world, at this point in history, are quite literally the result of human manipulation at a variety of levels.[1] In any case it doesn't seem too controversial to say that the world is always already mediated by subjectivity and through human history. There is no analytically separate metaphysical world outside us that would allow us, if we peeled away all the layers of history and of the human, to see true reality. To even think that one would experience a truer reality without our humanness is to have fallen completely into an absurd version of the metaphysical urge, and probably to have entered Kafka's insight that it signals an urge toward death. Marx avoids the metaphysical urge by stressing that the condition to know the world is to be able to interpret the world and to understand that interpretation is a laboring act involving mind and body. Interpretation is not merely a mental activity; rather it is a creation of our historical-biological selves, it is a sport.

When one casts off the metaphysical urge, one can stop chasing spooks and can talk about something real like alienation. Alienation occurs when one becomes separated from the world, others, or themselves. This separation is never simply an objective fact but is mediated by interpretive elements. As *DE* made clear, perception involves interpretation generally but we can further see what this means by focusing on concrete human labor as Marx articulated it. Marx articulated labor as a philosophical category. Marx's philosophy starts with the alienation of the worker and shows how

---

1 Ibid.

alienation fundamentally involves social relations between humans within society. This is a proto-communicative action point that Habermas has analytically clarified. Under conditions of alienation work turns into an alien and independent power over and against humans; it seems external to humans. Whereas un-alienated labor expresses human projects and actualizes them, alienated labor has dominating effects so that "the worker sinks to the level of a commodity and becomes indeed the most wretched of commodities[.]"[1] Under conditions of alienation, the worker experiences the world as fundamentally instrumental, and hence as domination.

Marx describes four aspects in which the modern worker is alienated. The first is "that the object which labour produces—labour's product— confronts it as something alien, as a power independent of the producer."[2] Objects that workers create are produced for the market, they are commodities, and they belong to the owner of the means of production. The worker cannot keep the object or creatively alter it or even use it as a means to his or her own survival. It is not the workers property. This circumstance is alienating because the worker is deprived of the very thing that the worker has transformed. "The alienation of the worker in his product means not only that his labour becomes an object, an external existence, but that it exists outside him, independently, as something alien to him, and that it becomes a power of its own confronting him; it means that the life which he has conferred on the object confronts him as something hostile and alien."[3] The product gains the illusion of a living entity. The product gains power over the worker. The worker cannot decide the form the product takes. The product is not for the worker's use, but for the capitalist's profit. All the worker gets from the product is a wage, not self-recognition or a sense of purpose and meaningfulness. The product provides a means to the worker's subsistence, but is not part of the worker; it does not express the worker's being. Human needs and human fulfillment's become secondary. The only important question about the product is "will it sell?" So even the capitalist will have an alienating relationship to the product because the product's value as a commodity will supersede and drown out any other qualities it may possess.

The second aspect of alienation that Marx analyzes is the act of production itself. When labor is not free, it produces active alienation. This has especially disastrous human effects because we labor for such an extensive part of our lives. Alienating labor is labor that is external to the worker and "therefore, he does not affirm himself but denies himself, does not feel content but unhappy, does not develop freely his physical

---

1 Marx (1978), 70.
2 Ibid., 71.
3 Ibid., 72.

and mental energy but mortifies his body and ruins his mind. The worker therefore only feels himself outside his work, and in his work feels outside himself. He is at home when he is not working, and when he is working he is not at home."[1] Under these conditions work does not directly satisfy a need. "Its alien character emerges clearly in the fact that as soon as no physical or other compulsion exists, labour is shunned like the plague."[2] This "external character of labour for the worker appears in the fact that it is not his own, but someone else's, that it does not belong to him, that in it he belongs, not to himself, but to another."[3] The ultimate result is "the loss of his self."[4]

The loss of a free human self results in the worker no longer feeling "freely active in any but his animal functions—eating, drinking, procreating, or at most in his dwelling and in dressing-up, etc.; and in his human functions he no longer feels himself to be anything but an animal. What is animal becomes human and what is human becomes animal."[5] The point here is not that human activities like eating and drinking are alienating in themselves, but rather that "in the abstraction which separates them from the sphere of all other human activity and turns them into sole and ultimate ends, they are animal."[6] When these other activities have to carry so much mental and psychological weight, it saps the human meaning from them and creates irrational attachments. Food, alcohol, and sex addictions grow more and more common in our society. Rather than a simple Friday night dinner out on the town, the rendezvous at California Pizza Kitchen turns into a Hegelian master–slave dialectic until being a server in America is one of the most dreaded jobs for too many today. Patrons are so alienated during their work hours that by the time they get to the restaurant they either take out their frustrations on those serving them, skimp on the tip, overindulge themselves, run up debt, or fall into a childlike frenzy just trying to capture the feeling that they are somebody and that all the labor they have been doing is worth it. Clearly if you need CPK, an Audi, or a "roll tide" chant to feel like somebody, society has become wrong society.

There's nothing wrong with enjoying dinner, your car, or your favorite sports team; but when these things and activities become metaphysical, so to speak, they become problematic. Marx is not a foundationalist; specific activities are not seen as alienating or freeing in themselves. Rather, their character depends on how they are structured and how they relate to other aspects of human existence. Marx thus contrasts alienating existence with a

---

1 Ibid., 74.
2 Ibid.
3 Ibid.
4 Ibid.
5 Ibid.
6 Ibid.

potential existence that can express itself in the world. If capitalism's social relations lead to "loss of self" then humans need to change the alienating social relations. Change begins by looking at the structure of capitalism and challenging a merely instrumental conception of labor.

For Marx, labor should concretize a sense of unity and coherence to one's life. The lack of creative and unifying labor is most salient in the case of a worker whose activity is outside the worker's control. "It is activity as suffering, strength as weakness, begetting as emasculating, the worker's own physical and mental energy, his personal life...is turned against him, neither depends on nor belongs to him."[1] The point here is that alienated labor prevents workers from creating lives that can unify their day-to-day activities with their ideas of the meaning and value of human life. Alienated labor gives workers a false epistemological experience and distorted ontological worldview. Rather than seeing themselves in their activity and seeing the necessary interconnectedness and mediation of the subject/object relation workers are unable to grasp the human contribution reflected in their activity, and in the object of creation, and so cannot experience the world as their world. Without this ability the metaphysical urge or nihilistic tendencies replace the human meaning.

A third aspect of alienation follows from the others: this is alienation of individuals concretely from other individuals. Our relations with others under conditions of alienation are such that "each man views the other in accordance with the standard and the position in which he finds himself as a worker."[2] Workers are clearly alienated from the owners of capital, but they are also alienated from fellow workers due to the scarcity of jobs and the competitive nature of the modern economy. How many workers dream of winning the lottery, partly so they can finally get some financial relieve, but just as motivating, is the dream of being able to tell their boss to go shove it. Still, owners of business are not just the bad guys. Today many capitalists are also striving to create better, more meaningful lives, and just trying to survive in the world they found themselves in. But of course they cannot help but be alienated from their workers. If technology makes it so that workers are not needed, they must get rid of the workers. If they can find cheaper labor, of course, they will hire the cheaper labor. They must also battle constantly against other capitalists in the competition for finite markets. The progress of modernity has ironically also pushed alienation into ever more spheres of life.

The final and most important aspect of alienation for our enquiry is alienation from what Marx, following Feuerbach, calls "species being."

1 Ibid., 75.
2 Ibid., 77.

Species being for Marx refers to the manner in which the individual "adopts the species as his object."[1] Marx's point seems to be that individuals know that there is a human species of which the individual is a part and that individuals are conscious of themselves as a human among others past, present, and future. So if individuals are alienated from their species being, in the sense that they lose the insight of our mutual interdependence and in fact tend to view most others in competitive and hostile terms, then the individuals will not be able to concretely live and experience the community of which they are necessarily a part. One will not see past the reified immediacy of things nor understand how what he or she is, as an individual, is a work of history and necessarily intersubjective. Consequently, even if this individual has rejected the notion of meaning coming from above, this individual alienated from his or her species being may mistakenly believe that he or she alone is the origin of values and of meaning. This belief may be too daunting and as such may open the door to the nihilism that Nietzsche predicted. The suggestion here is that recognizing oneself as a "species being" is necessary for overcoming the metaphysical urge and nihilism and moving toward the creation of rational meaning.

By making labor into the central category of both his epistemology and his social theory, Marx draws our attention to the fact that humanity is through and through the product of human labor and the way labor is organized will have philosophical implications in determining what our lives will amount to. The philosophical starting point is to recognize that we are alienated from ourselves when we fail to recognize our common humanity, when we are unable to see the world as our world, as our product, and when our own activity appears as an alien power over and against us. Without the recognition of our common humanity we will be unable to balance the intrinsic and instrumental aspects of rationality, and we will be unable to unleash and seize the intersubjective truth of the human condition. Just like we are connected to others we are connected to earlier parts of ourselves. The early Marx of the *Manuscripts* connects to the later Marx of *Das Kapital* in that the latter can be seen to extend the critique of alienation into an explicit critique of the metaphysical urge. This is accomplished via the theory of the fetishism of commodities. The fetishism of commodities is Marx's idiom for expressing the metaphysical urge and his critique of the fetishism of commodities can be read as a historical and concrete critique of the metaphysical urge.

---

1 Ibid., 75.

Capital Fetish

In *Capital* Marx offers an account of alienation that he articulates through the labor theory of value. Marx's analysis shows that labor is the paramount source of value. It follows, then, that capital, as labor's antithesis, owes its existence to labor. Capital exists because human labor produced the value. It is the labor of past work embodied specifically in the capitalist's wealth and concretely throughout society that now exists in the environment that is our world today. Marx's analysis in *Capital* can be read as having the same structure as his earlier analysis of alienation (in the *1844 Manuscripts*)[1]. In *Capital*, the basic point is that the worker's labor is objectified, and the object, in the form of capital, turns into an independent and alien force over and against the worker. *Capital* is not a simple attack on money but rather it is a critique of the aspects of domination that internally arise in a capitalist society. We will briefly detail his argument.

In *Capital* the analysis begins at the level of a commodity. According to Marx there are two salient dimensions to a commodity: use-value and exchange value. Use-value refers to a thing's utility. The use-value of a product is the properties that make it effectual. Use-value captures the qualitative aspects of an object. The usefulness of iron, for example, stems from the specific qualities of iron.[2] Exchange-value at first glance may seem like a quantitative measurement. Yet, actually it is a measurement of socially necessary labor time. We do exchange things, primarily through the medium of money, and ideally the exchange is fair. What determines fairness? Following Adam Smith Marx argues that exchange-value has its origins in labor. We need not go into the subtleties of Smith's and Marx's views on the labor theory of value, but the relevant point for our inquiry is that in both cases a commodity is first of all the product or result of human labor and this labor primarily is the source of its value. The problem is that under conditions of capitalist production labor does not appear as the source of value that it is. In fact, the value of the commodity appears as a natural fact about it, an objective fact independent of human action. What is really a relation between humans, with its necessarily implicit cooperation of laboring subjects, here appears only in the distorted and alienated form of a relation between things. The values of objects have their source in human labor but this connection to us has been lost. It is important to recognize that Marx is making an epistemological, not an economic point. The value of commodities (reflected more or less in their price) cannot be delinked from human social organization and yet in the modern world we generally

---

1 See Althusser's *For Marx* for a very different interpretation.
2 Marx, *Capital* Vol. I, in *The Marx–Engels Reader* (New York: Norton, 1978), pp. 302-08.

consider value as somehow capturing what an object is intrinsically worth. We often speak of the "law of the market" as if there was something external to us that is controlling the exchange values. In the so-called free market values seem to be more closely linked to the objects themselves than to human labor. Marx wants us to consider the social and political ramifications of this peculiar phenomenon. He thinks the result of this epistemological error is that human actions are expressed as actions of objects or actions of a market above, beyond, and separate from human control. The error structurally mirrors the logic of the metaphysical urge and has the power of metaphysical truth.

This state of affairs reaches its climax in the phenomenon Marx calls the "fetishism of commodities." A commodity, that "very queer thing, abounding in metaphysical subtleties and theological niceties"[1] is a result of a human, laboring world, it is not a naturally occurring thing, but is simply a product of human exchange. This, again, is not to say that markets and the modern economy are not complicated and complex. But the point is that when exchange-value takes precedent over use-value (because of capital's social organization) subjects and objects take on an abstract and mythical meaning. The human meaning gets obscured as capitalism creates a false representation of the dialectic. The representation is false because even though the labor that produces a commodity is implicitly social and cooperative it does not appear that way. The social consequences are alienation and the political ones are inequalities in power. A commodity is produced to satisfy the needs of others, but private property and exchange conceal this sociality. The result of this concealment is a type of alienation that we have seen Marx here calls the "fetishism of commodities." Commodities have been granted mystical powers and this benefits some classes and some individuals more than others. Again, we see that labor, which should express human powers, has turned into alienation. It is alienation because it separates us from something whose authors we are. As such we can say capitalism is structured like religion, enlightenment is myth.

The Sporting Life

With the concepts of species being and the critique of the fetishism of commodities, Marx has moved beyond the expressive notion that overcoming alienation consists simply in the worker seeing himself in his work environment that Habermas accused him of. Rather, Marx is claiming that labor, in the modern world, is a communal practice and that overcoming alienation is when we see ourselves in our products, activity, relationships, and when we see that these express the agreements we have come to

---

1 Ibid., 319.

communicatively about our values. Marx here highlights the fact that individuals are always already situated within history and social structures and connected to a larger human community that is at bottom cooperative. Not to see this is a form of alienation. When one is alienated from his or her species, it "turns...the life of the species into a means of individual life."[1] Against this result, humans need to recognize that: "Conscious life-activity directly distinguishes man from animal life-activity. It is just because of this that he is a species being. Or it is only because he is a species being that he is a Conscious Being, i.e., that his own life is an object for him."[2] "In tearing away from man the object of his production, therefore, estranged labor tears from him his species-life, his real objectivity as a member of the species, and transforms his advantage over animals into the disadvantage that his inorganic body, nature, is taken away from him."[3]

The worker's alienation then turns out to be of larger consequence. Labor is not simply instrumental, rather, in our globalized modernity, it is necessarily intertwined with what Habermas calls communicative action. Today labor itself is not simply or foremost about manipulating an object. Today's labor is not just manufacturing, but service centered, information driven, and fundamentally involves subjects interacting with other subjects all of whom must assume a communicative framework for the system to function. It's still fashionable to think that game theory captures human interaction but in the concrete, human world most of us know this is not true—and where it is, it probably shouldn't be. For modern labor is not a strategic game. It is a part of a complicated structure that we need to function rationally if we are to preserve ourselves and create good selves. It is not something that we should be playing games with. Further it is not fundamentally about subject/ objects relations. Overall, we have conquered scarcity, we do understand nature, and we are reproducing our material lives. The question, at this point in history, is not how we can control objects to survive, but rather it is why we are distributing our resources and human capital in such a way that we are not actualizing ourselves. Whether we are conscious of it or not, modern labor is social and intersubjective, and it expresses, reflects, and recreates the meanings and values we hold dear. If this is true, then the meanings and values need to have come from a communicative process. For if they are driven by strategic forces, then not only will workers not be able to express themselves through their labor, but their ability to come to communicative agreement and understanding will be distorted throughout the lifeworld. The result will be a lack of human meaning and reconciliation both inside and outside work. The result will be a wrong society.

1 Ibid., 75.
2 Ibid., 76.
3 Ibid., 76-77.

In wrong society the metaphysical urge becomes a fetish. Yet when we can see past this fetish, when we break its spell, we can see that: "The object of labour is, therefore, the objectification of man's species life: for he duplicates himself not only, as in consciousness, intellectually, but also actively, in reality, and therefore he contemplates himself in a world that he has created."[1] The point is that the creation of individuals occurs within a larger, communicative species narrative. Marx is trying to "uncongeal" our individual lives to show the mediations and collective processes that make our individual lives possible in the first place. It is human history that sets the terms and conditions of individuals. There is nothing magical or outside us that is pulling the strings. Rather, without the labor of humanity up to this point our individual lives would not be our lives. This critique suggests that modernity needs to cast off the metaphysical urge, stop Tebowing, and connect with real others. Not acknowledging that one's individual success is predicated on and only possible because of countless others and because of human history would be like the quarterback and running backs on a football team not acknowledging the role the offensive line plays in their success. Could you imagine your team winning the Super Bowl without an offensive line? That's not really even intelligible, but we can image winning without a God watching. The offensive line deserves the championship rings as much as the quarterback does. To try to deny them rings because they didn't throw any touchdown passes or rush for any scores would be to completely miss their contribution, and to misunderstand the game.[2]

In the world of global capitalism, labor is like the offensive line of a football team. Both are driving the success and both are intimately connected to the meanings and values possible at our time. The running back who thanks God rather than the line after a score is under the sway of a ridiculous fetish and has reduced other human beings to their instrumental value.

The recognition of the communicative and social aspects of labor puts Marx in a better position than others in the tradition to fruitfully challenge a purely instrumental notion of labor. Marx lived at a time when the philosopher could directly see how labor was driving the emerging modern world. Today, watch any excellent football team and you can directly see how the offensive line drives the success of the offense. But where the great quarterbacks reward their linemen, our society treats most laborers like second class citizens. So at Marx's time he could say without exaggeration that: "labour produces for the rich wonderful things—but for the worker it produces privation. It produces palaces—but for the worker, hovels.

---

1 Ibid., 76.
2 For a good article on the importance of the offensive line, see the following article.   http://www.csnphilly.com/blog/700-level/offensive-line-most-impor-tant-position-football

It produces beauty—but for the worker, deformity. It replaces labour by machines—but some of the workers it throws back to a barbarous type of labour, and the other workers it turns into machines. It produces intelligence—but for the worker idiocy, cretinism."[1] Even if workers in advanced industrial nations no longer live in hovels, it is clear that too many laboring citizens are under recognized and undervalued.

Modernity in many ways then is like the NFL. It seems to be good and bad, to be progress and decline, at the same time. Football is an amazingly complicated and exhilarating sport. It requires great individuals and sophisticated teamwork. It can be a thing of beauty, art, and solidarity and it can be brutal, corrupt, and sadistic. At some point it may be time to give up football. We may be getting to that point in human history. Today's athletes are stronger, faster, and more powerful than ever before. We have new, worrisome knowledge and understanding of concussions. And the obsessive focus on profit at the expense of players, fans, cities, and human values might signal that it's time to move on to something else, or to alter the game radically.

Modernity also, as driven by capitalism, may need to rethink its attachment to an economic system predicated on class distinctions, alienation, and exploitation. For the promise of modernity was a promise of freedom and happiness, yet in our global capitalist world more and more people are finding it difficult to form free and meaningful lives. Clearly in the modern world there are multifarious opportunities for self-formation and yet, at the same time, the world appears alienating and meaningless. Capitalism promotes human development and then crushes all but a few winners at the top. But life is not sports. There is not supposed to be just one winner. One of the intriguing things about sports is that we get to see what happens when you can have only one winner. The NCAA basketball tournament is wonderful for this very reason. But, again, life is not sports. In life the goal should be to have as many winners as possible. My win should be consistent with your win. We all live our individual lives and have different visions of the good life. No one is fighting for the exact same trophy, but in wrong society this fact gets mystified. The instrumental world tries to trick us into thinking there can be only one gold medal just like the metaphysical urge tries to trick us into thinking there can be only one eternal truth. This sinister side of both myth and enlightenment denies individuals their true image. This regressive urge we should not root for, we need not abide.

---

1 *The Marx-Engels Reader*, 73.

I'm Coming Home

While in Miami, of all places, LeBron James became aware of his own image. James is a magnificent athlete, the best basketball player of his generation and the greatest in the world today. Still, as a poor kid from Akron, OH, brought up by a struggling single mom, it's been a difficult journey. His talent was obvious from an early age and by the time he was ready to go to high school he was already being highly recruited from every direction, by the most sacred and the most profane. Still, he was never afraid to take chances. Instead of making the safe choice and going to the local public high school, he ventured to an almost exclusively white, private school.[1] But he never tried to do it alone. He's always been a team player, both on and off the court, a great passer, and an unselfish individual. Despite the early and constant pressure—ESPN even televised one of his high school games—he didn't fold, and his pre-NBA career was legendary.

The legend only grew as the Cleveland Cavaliers drafted him with their first pick and he led the team to the NBA Championship finals without much talent surrounding him. He gave the city seven years before deciding it was time to move on. Basketball is a team sport and nobody wins it all without great teammates, nobody: not Kobe, not Michael, not Shaq.

His hometown hated him for leaving. Fans burned his jersey. The owner, Dan Gilbert, penned, and made public, a spiteful rate against his former star. LeBron himself was not completely innocent. Although he had a right to leave, and probably needed to leave to achieve his goals, he made some awkward missteps (that most young men probably would have made in that situation). The less said about "The Decision" the better. In Miami he had some trials and tribulations but ultimately took his greatness to still another level. Whether it was in the NBA or on Team USA, it was clear that a newer, better version of LeBron the man had emerged. He achieved instrumental success, his character grew, solidified, and unified, and by the time he exited Miami there was no doubt he was "King James."

But success without reconciliation is not enlightenment. On July 17th 2014, LeBron James told the world "I'm coming home."[2] Now he's back in Cleveland, married to his high school sweetheart, has some kids, and is trying to have success and happiness, meaning and reconciliation. As he put it: "When I left Cleveland, I was on a mission, I was seeking championships, and we won two. But Miami already knew that feeling. Our city hasn't had that feeling in a long, long, long time. My goal is still to win as many titles as possible, no question. But what's most important for me is bringing

---

1 He transferred with three teammates.
2 He announced this on his website.

one trophy back to Northeast Ohio."[1] Going back to Cleveland, like living without the metaphysical urge, provokes ambiguity. Going back, and facing the world as a human world, full of contradictory truths, awaits him. James is much wiser now and undoubtedly carries with him the wisdom that the only certainty is lack of certainty. In an uncertain human world, it is best not to act alone. "To make the move I needed the support of my wife and my mom, who can be very tough," "The letter from Dan Gilbert, the booing of the Cleveland fans, the jerseys being burned—seeing all that was hard for them. My emotions were more mixed. It was easy to say, 'OK, I don't want to deal with these people ever again.' But then you think about the other side. What if I were a kid who looked up to an athlete, and that athlete made me want to do better in my own life, and then he left? How would I react? I've met with Dan, face to face, man to man. We've talked it out. Everybody makes mistakes. I've made mistakes as well. Who am I to hold a grudge?"[2]

The intrinsic and instrumental hang in dialectical balance as LeBron James tries to make Cleveland the homeland, to wrest it from myth, and make it and his evolving self what they are capable of becoming. There's no guarantee that the move back to Cleveland will turn out for the best; it's a risky move, full of contingent factors beyond any individual's control. The move back won't be easy and success will not happen overnight. Still, it's a rational move, both intrinsically and instrumentally so. With his new team, in Cleveland, he's giving himself perhaps the best opportunity to win, and he's connecting with his community, and he's rooting his potentially best self. He's not trying to do it alone, not trying to merely go back; he is trying to bring everyone forward. He's coming home as home is coming to him.

1 http://www.usatoday.com/story/sports/nba/cavaliers/2014/07/11/lebron-james-return-cleveland-cavaliers-contract-miami-heat/12444643/
2 Ibid.

Acknowledgements

Thanks to Georgia Warnke, Shane Hillyer, Christine Duvergé, Jay Conway, Thomas Donovan, Jim Davis, and Wendy Walczak for the conversations and feedback that helped make this book possible. Thank you to Mt. San Jacinto College for my one semester sabbatical. And a special thank you to my parents for their love and support.

BIBLIOGRAPHY

Adorno, Theodor. *Aesthetic Theory*. Robert Hullot-Kentor, trans. Minneapolis. Minnesota Press. 1997.

_____. *Minima Moralia*. E. F. N. Jephcott, trans. London. Verso. 1994.

_____. *Negative Dialectics*. E. B. Ashton, trans. New York. Continuum. 1992.

American Beauty. Sam Mendes. Dreamworks. 1999. DVD.

Arato, Andrew. "Lukács's Theory of Reification." *Telos* 11. Spring 1972.

Arato, Andrew and Paul Breines. *The Young Lukács and the Origins of Western Marxism*. New York. Seabury Press. 1979.

Badiou, Alain. *Theory of the Subject*, Bruno Bostells, trans. London. Continuum. 2009.

Berman, Marshall. *Adventures in Marxism*. London. Verso. 1999.

Bernstein, J. M. "Lukács Wake: Praxis, Presence, and Metaphysics." *Lukács Today*. Rockmore. 1988.

_____. *The Philosophy of the Novel*. Minneapolis. University of Minnesota Press. 1984.

Bleacher Report. bleacherreport.com/articles/1169405-paul-pierces-tebowing-diss-in-game-2-proves-some-nba-stars-never-grow-up.

Brudney, Daniel. *Marx's Attempt to Leave Philosophy*. Cambridge. Harvard University Press. 1998.

Callinicos, Alex. *Against Postmodernism*. New York. Saint Martin's Press. 1989.

_____. *Social Theory*. New York. New York University Press. 1999.

CBS Sports. www.cbssports.com/nba/blog/eye-on-basketball/18927132.

Christian Science Monitor. http://www.csmonitor.com/USA/Sports/2012/ 0112/ Poll-God-helps-Tim-Tebow-win-football-games.-Does-Tim-Tebow-agree.

Cohen, Jean, L. and Andrew Arato. *Civil Society and Political Theory*. Cambridge. The MIT Press. 1992.

Crimes and Misdemeanors. Woody Allen. MGM. 1989. DVD.

Dante, Alighieri. *The Inferno*. John Ciardi, trans. New York. Signet. 2001.

Davis, Walter. *Death's Dream Kingdom*. London. Pluto Press. 2006.

Descartes, *Meditations on First Philosophy*. Donald A. Cress, trans. Indianapolis. Hackett Publishing.1993.

Eagleton, Terry. *Culture and the Death of God*. New Haven. Yale University Press. 2014.

_____. *Ideology*. New York. Verso. 1991.

_____. *On Evil*. New Haven. Yale University Press. 2010.

_____. *Reason, Faith, and Revolution*. New Haven. Yale University Press. 2009.

ESPN.   http://espn.go.com/nba/story/_/id/11105717/sad-last-chapter-donald-sterling-life.

_____. http://scores.espn.go.com/nfl/recap?gameId=320108007.

Feenberg. Andrew. *Lukács, Marx and the Sources of Critical Theory*. Oxford. Martin Robertson. 1981.

Foster, Roger. "Dialectic of Enlightenment as Genealogy Critique." *Telos* 2001 (120):73-93. 2001.

Fraser, Nancy and Axel Honneth. *Redistribution or Recognition*. London. Verso. 2003

Fraser, Nancy. *Scales of Justice*. Columbia. Columbia University Press. 2010.

Freud, Sigmund. *Civilization and Its Discontents*. New York. W. W. Norton. 1989.

_____. *The Future of an Illusion*. New York. W. W. Norton. 1989.

Foucault, Michel. *Discipline and Punish*. Alan Sheridan, trans. New York. Vintage Books. 1977.

Fukuyama, Francis. *America at the Crossroads*. New Haven. Yale University Press. 2006.

_____. *The End of History and the Last Man*. New York. Free Press. 2006.

Gadamer, Hans-Georg. *Truth and Method*. Joel Weinsheimer and Donald G. Marshall, trans. New York. Continuum. 1996.

Geuss, Raymond. *Outside Ethics*. Princeton. Princeton University Press. 2005.

_____. *Politics and the Imagination*. Princeton. Princeton University Press. 2010.

Gray, John. *The Immortalization Commission*. New York. Farrar, Straus and Giroux. 2011.

_____. *Straw Dogs*. New York. Farrar, Straus and Giroux. 2003.

Habermas, Jürgen. *Between Facts and Norms*. William Rehg, trans. Cambridge. MIT Press. 1996.

_____. *Between Naturalism and Religion*. Cambridge. Polity Press. 2008.

_____. Habermas and Joseph Ratzinger. *The Dialectics of Secularization*. San Francisco. Ignatius Press. 2005.

_____. *Justification and Application*. Ciaran P. Cronin, trans. Cambridge. MIT Press. 1993.

_____. *Moral Consciousness and Communicative Action*. Christian Lenhardt and Shierry Weber Nicholsen, trans. Cambridge. The MIT Press. 1991.

_____. *On Society and Politics*, ed. Steven Seidman. Boston. Beacon Press. 1989.

_____. *The Philosophical Discourse of Modernity*. Frederick G. Lawrence, trans. Cambridge. MIT Press. 1992.

_____. *The Structural Transformation of the Public Sphere*. Thomas Burger, trans. Cambridge. The MIT Press. 1993.

_____. *The Theory of Communicative Action*, 2 vols. Thomas McCarthy, trans. Boston. Beacon Press, 1984 and 1987.

Hall, Stuart. *Modernity*. Cambridge. Blackwell. 1996.

Harvey, David. *The Condition of Postmodernity*. Cambridge. Blackwell Press. 1990.

_____. *The Limits To Capital*. New York. Verso. 1999.

Hegel, G. W. F., *Elements of the Philosophy of Right*. H. B. Nisbet, trans. Cambridge. Cambridge University Press. 1991.

_____. *The Encyclopaedia Logic*. Indianapolis. Hacket Publishing. 1991.

_____. *Phenomenology of Spirit*. A. V. Miller, trans. Oxford. Oxford University Press. 1977.

Heidegger, Martin. *Being and Time*. San Francisco. HarperSan Francisco 1962.

Homer. *Iliad*. Stanley Lombardo, trans. Cambridge. Hacket Publishing. 1997.

_____. *Odyssey*. Stanley Lombardo, trans. Cambridge. Hacket Publishing. 2000.

Honneth, Axel. *Reification*. New York. Oxford. 2008.

Horkheimer, Max and Theodor W. Adorno. *Dialectic of Enlightenment*. Edmund Jephcott, trans. Stanford. Stanford University Press. 2002.

Horkheimer, Max. *Eclipse of Reason*. London. Continuum. 2004.

Huffington Post. http://www.huffingtonpost.com/2012/06/18/fight-church-documentary-_n_1605983.html.

Ingram, David. *Habermas and the Dialectic of Reason*. London. Yale University Press. 1987.

Jameson, Fredric. *Marxism and Form*. New Jersey. Princeton University Press. 1971.

_____. *The Political Unconscious*. New York. Cornell University Press. 1981.

Jarvis, Simon. *Adorno*. New York. Routledge. 1998.

Jay, Martin. *Adorno*. Cambridge. Harvard University Press. 1984.

_____. *The Dialectical Imagination*. Boston. Little, Brown and Company. 1973.

_____. "Habermas and Modernism," in *Habermas and Modernity*, ed. Richard J. Bernstein. Cambridge. MIT Press. 1991.

_____. *Marxism and Totality*. Berkeley. University of California Press. 1984.

Kafka, *The Diary*. http://notesfromaroom.com/2010/07/27/kafka-quotes-2/.

_____. *The Metamorphosis*. Joyce Crick, trans. Oxford. Oxford University Press. 2009.

Kant, Immanuel. *Critique of Pure Reason*. Norman Kemp Smith, trans. New York. St. Martin's Press. 1965.

_____. What is Enlightenment?" in *Foundations of the Metaphysics of Morals*. New Jersey. Prentice-Hall. 1997.

Kellner, Douglas. *Critical Theory, Marxism and Modernity*. Baltimore. John Hopkins University Press. 1989.

Kierkegaard, Soren. *Fear and Trembling*. London. Oxford University Press. 1939.

Kundera, Molan. *The Art of the Novel*. Linda Asher, trans. New York. HarperCollins. 2000.

_____. *The Curtain*. Linda Asher, trans. New York. Harper. 2006.

_____. *Ignorance*. Linda Asher, trans. New York. Perennial. 2002.

_____. *Immortality*. Peter Kussi, trans. New York. HarperPerennial. 1991.

Lefebvre, Henri. *Critique of Everyday Life*. John Moore, trans. New York. Verso. 1991.

Lukács, Georg. *A Defense of History and Class Consciousness*. Esther Leslie, trans. London. Verso. 2000.

_____. *History and Class Consciousness*. Rodney Livingstone, trans. Cambridge. MIT Press. 1971.

_____. *Marxism and Human Liberation*. New York. Dell Publishing, 1973.

_____. *Soul and Form*. Anna Bostock, trans. Cambridge. The MIT Press. 1971.

_____. *The Theory of the Novel*. Anna Bostock, trans. Cambridge. MIT Press. 1999.

Mandel, Ernest. *Late Capitalism*. Joris De Bres, trans. New York. Verso. 1972.

Marcuse, Herbert. *Eros and Civilization*. Boston. Beacon Press. 1966.

_____. *One-Dimensional Man*. Boston. Beacon Press. 1964.

_____. *Reason and Revolution: Hegel and the Rise of Social Theory*. Boston. 1960.

Marx, Karl. *Capital* vol. one. Ben Fowkes, trans. New York. Vintage Books. 1977.

Marx, Karl and Frederick Engels. *The Communist Manifesto*. Samuel Moore, trans. New York. Washington Square Press. 1964.

_____. *Economic and Philosophic Manuscripts of 1844*. New York. Prometheus. 1988.

_____. *The Marx-Engels Reader*. New York. W. W. Norton. 1978.

McCarthy, Cormac. *The Road*. New York. Vintage. 2006.

Nehamas, Alexander. *The Art of Living*. Berkeley. University of California Press. 1998.

_____. *Nietzsche: Life as Literature*. Cambridge. Harvard University Press. 1985.

_____. "Nietzsche, modernity, aestheticism." Bernd Magnus and Kathleen M. Higgins, *The Cambridge Companion to Nietzsche*. Cambridge. Cambridge University Press. 1996.

_____. *Only a Promise of Happiness*. Princeton. Princeton University Press. 2007.

_____. *Virtues of Authenticity*. New Jersey. Princeton University Press. 1999.

Nietzsche, Frederick. *The Portable Nietzsche*. Walter Kaufmann, trans. New York. Penguin Books. 1982.

_____. *Twilight of the Idols*. Richard Polt, trans. Indianapolis. Hackett Publishing. 1997.

Nussbaum, Martha. *Love's Knowledge*. New York. Oxford University Press. 1990.

Offe, Claus. *Contradictions of the Welfare State*, ed. John Keane. Cambridge. The MIT Press. 1993.

Ollman, Bertell, *Alienation*. Cambridge. Cambridge University Press. 1976.

Onfray, Michel. *Atheist Manifesto*. Jeremy Leggatt, trans. New York. Arcade Publishing. 2007.

Pinker, Steven. *The Better Angels of our Nature*. New York. Penguin. 2012.

Plantinga, Alvin. *Where the Conflict Really Lies*. Oxford. Oxford University Press. 2011.

Plato. *The Trial and Death of Socrates*. Indianapolis. Hackett Publishing. 2000.

Poe, Edgar Allan. *The Annotated Tales of Edgar Allan Poe*. New York. Avenel Books. 1986.

Popdust. http://popdust.com/2013/04/22/daft-punk-pharrell-get-lucky-lyrics-meaning/.

Rasmussen, David. *Reading Habermas*. Cambridge. Basil Blackwell, 1991.

Rorty, Richard. *Contingency, Irony, and Solidarity*. Cambridge. Cambridge University Press. 1989.

Roy, Olivier, *Holy Ignorance*. New York. Columbia University Press. 2010.

Ryan, Christopher and Cacilda Jethá. *Sex at Dawn*. New York. Harper. 2010.

Sade, Marquis, de. *Juliette*. New York. Grove Press. 1994.

_____. *Justine, or the Misfortunes of Virtue*. Oxford. Oxford University Press. 2013.

Sartre, Jean-Paul. *Existentialism and Human Emotions*. New York. Citadel Press. 1985.

_____. *Literature & Existentialism*. New York. Citadel. 1977.

Schopenhauer, Arthur. *The World as Weill and Representation*. E. F. J. Payne, trans. New York. Dover Publications. 1969.

Shakespeare, William. *The Complete Works*. New York. The Viking Press. 1986.

Smiley, Tavis and Cornel West. *The Rich and the Rest of Us*. New York. Smileybooks. 2012.

Taylor, Charles, *Hegel*. Cambridge. Cambridge University Press. 1975.

USA Today. http://www.usatoday.com/story/sports/nba/cavaliers/2014/07/11/lebron-james-return-cleveland-cavaliers-contract-miami-heat/12444643/.

Village Voice. blogs.villagevoice.com/music/2013/09/nile_rodgers_get_lucky.php.

Vogel, Steven. *Against Nature*. Albany. State University of New York Press. 1996.

_____. "Marx and Alienation from Nature." *Social Theory and Practice*, Vol. 14, No. 3, Fall 1988.

Warnke, Georgia. "Communicative Rationality and Cultural Values." *The Cambridge Companion to Habermas*, Ed. Stephen K. White. Cambridge. Cambridge University Press. 1995.

_____. *Gadamer*. Stanford. Stanford University Press. 1987.

_____. *Legitimate Differences: Interpretation in the Abortion Controversy and Other Public Debates*. Berkeley. University of California Press. 1999.

Wiggershaus, Rolf. *The Frankfurt School*. Michael Robertson, trans. Cambridge. The MIT Press. 1994.

Wikipedia. http://en.wikipedia.org/wiki/3:16_Game

Wolin, Richard. *The Frankfurt School Revisited*. New York. Routledge. 2006.

Žižek, Slavoj. How to Read Lacan.

_____. *Less Than Nothing*. London. Verso. 2012.

_____. *Living in End Times*. London. Verso. 2010.

_____. *The Puppet and the Dwarf*. Cambridge. The MIT Press. 2003.

_____. *The Sublime Object of Ideology*. London. Verso. 1999.

INDEX

T

Tebow, Tim, 1-7, 9, 21, 30, 46, 48, 49, 51, 52
Thomas, Demaryius, 1, 78, 133, 134, 155, 159

V

Vogel, Steven, 27, 133, 141, 162

W

Weber, Max, 134, 159
Winters, Tex, 47
Wittgenstein, Ludwig, 59, 67
Wolin, Richard, 38, 162
Woods, Tiger, 49

Z

Zimmerman, George, 104, 105

Ž

Žižek, Slavoj, 29, 34, 57, 58, 61, 162

Printed in the United States
By Bookmasters